*Some books entertain, others inform, but Unsung* ▮▮▮ *does something rarer: it preserves the lived wis*▮▮▮ *turned challenge into legacy. These stories of women entrepreneurs are raw, resilient, and revelatory, told with the kind of honesty that cuts through the noise of business clichés. Having worked with hundreds of authors and having seen firsthand the power of women's narratives in business, I can say this: the voices here matter. They don't just inspire; they validate. They give shape to the collective story of women who build, rebuild, and lift others as they climb. A must-read for entrepreneurs, professionals, and anyone reflecting on their own journey.*

Ania Kubicki
ANGLES Communications
NAWBO PHX President 2022–23

*Unsung Heroines of Business is a powerful tribute to women who lead with grit, grace, and unwavering purpose. Each story is a reminder that courage often lives quietly behind the scenes, and that true leadership is forged in moments of doubt, resilience, and bold reinvention. Debra Corrie has curated a collection that is both deeply personal and universally inspiring. This is a must-read for anyone who believes in the transformative power of women in business.*

Farica Chang
CEO, Anderson Technologies

*Feeling stuck? Read this book—again and again. Each chapter delivers hope and a jolt of courage for leaders navigating change, personally and professionally. These stories feel like one-on-one mentorship sessions, turning wounds into wisdom and setbacks into strategy. With deep principles that resonate at home and in the boardroom, this anthology offers real-life examples and practical ways to rise.*

Tim Van Mieghem
Founding Partner of The ProAction Group

Author of *Shocking Profit: Cash in on Your Company's Hidden Value, Grow Leaders, and Spark a Transformation That Changes Everything*
(available October 28, 2025)

*Don't expect another collection of overnight success stories.* Unsung Heroines of Business *documents the unglamorous reality of building enterprises while juggling crises most entrepreneurs never discuss publicly. These women started companies during divorces, health emergencies, and economic downturns. What emerges isn't inspiration fluff but real business and life intelligence. It will help you lead teams when you're barely holding it together yourself. The tactical details matter. You'll discover specific strategies for bootstrapping without venture capital, building customer loyalty through authentic relationships, and scaling operations with limited resources. This is a field manual for anyone serious about growth without safety nets.*

Cynthia Kirkpatrick
Senior Advisor, Moneta

Unsung Heroines of Business *is a powerful tapestry of grit, grace, and practical wisdom. These voices invite you to keep going when the ground shifts, to follow your bliss with both feet on the floor, to turn service, faith, and community into sustainable leadership. From military chapels to startup boardrooms to immigrant entrepreneurship, each story rings true and offers a usable lesson. I finished each chapter feeling seen, energized, and ready to mentor the next woman in line.*

Heather Frigaard
CEO • AI Pioneer • Servant Leader, LIM Marketing

WOMEN WHO BREAK THROUGH BARRIERS,
EXCEL IN BUSINESS, AND INSPIRE
THE NEXT GENERATION

# UNSUNG
# HEROINES
## OF BUSINESS

A COMPILATION BY
# DEBI CORRIE

**Unsung Heroines of Business**
Women Who Break Through Barriers, Excel in Business,
and Inspire the Next Generation
Debi Corrie

Published by DJC Media, LLC, St Louis, MO
Copyright ©2025 Debi Corrie
All rights reserved.

Limit of Liability/Disclaimer of Warranty: While the publisher and author have used their best efforts in preparing this book, they make no representations or warranties with respect to the accuracy or completeness of the contents of this book and specifically disclaim any implied warranties of merchantability or fitness for a particular purpose. No warranty may be created or extended by sales representatives or written sales materials. The advice and strategies contained herein may not be suitable for your situation. You should consult with a professional where appropriate. Neither the publisher nor the author shall be liable for any loss of profit or any other commercial damages, including but not limited to special, incidental, consequential, or other damages.

The product information and advice provided (in this book) are intended for general informational purposes only. The author and publisher of this book have made every effort to ensure that the content is accurate and up-to-date at the time of publication. However, they make no representations or warranties of any kind, express or implied, about the completeness, accuracy, reliability, suitability, or availability of the information, products, or services contained in this book for any purpose.

Project Management and Book Design: Davis Creative, LLC, DavisCreativePublishing.com
Cover Design: Missy Asikainen
Editor: Katie Gearin

Publisher's Cataloging-in-Publication
Names: Corrie, Debi, compiler.
Title: Unsung heroines of business : women who break through barriers, excel in business, and inspire the next generation / a compilation by Debi Corrie.
Description: St Louis, MO : DJC Media, LLC, [2025]
Identifiers: LCCN: 2025917467 | ISBN: 9781735990330 (paperback) | 9781735990347 (ebook)
Subjects: LCSH: Businesswomen--Anecdotes. | Leadership--Anecdotes. | Self-actualization (Psychology) in women--Anecdotes. | Work-life balance--Anecdotes. | Glass ceiling (Employment discrimination)--Anecdotes. | BISAC: BUSINESS & ECONOMICS / Women in Business. | BUSINESS & ECONOMICS / Leadership. | BUSINESS & ECONOMICS / Entrepreneurship.
Classification: LCC: HD6053 .U57 2025 | DDC: 658.11082--dc23

**ATTENTION CORPORATIONS, UNIVERSITIES, COLLEGES, AND PROFESSIONAL ORGANIZATIONS:** Quantity discounts are available on bulk purchases of this book for educational, gift purposes, or as premiums for increasing magazine subscriptions or renewals. Special books or book excerpts can also be created to fit specific needs. For information, please contact Debi Corrie, DJC Media LLC, debi@debicorrie.com

# DEDICATION

*Dedicated to all the Unsung Heroines in this book,*
*the people who supported them on their journeys,*
*and the courage and persistence of women.*
*It has been my honor and privilege to curate*
Unsung Heroines of Business.
*Your stories will inspire the next generation of heroines.*

# TABLE OF CONTENTS

*Continued on next page*

## Introduction

"Thank you, Debi, for the path you paved." The person on the phone said these very powerful words to me while I was traveling to a networking event. It stopped me for a second, and I really didn't understand what the person was saying to me. "Can you explain that to me, please?" I asked. She elaborated by saying, "You started out in transportation, an industry that was mostly male-dominated, and now other women are in that industry because of the path you paved. You made the way for other people like me to work in male-dominated industries."

I'd never really thought about any of this. Never thought I was a great adventurer. Never thought I would be forging a path for the young women that followed me. But what I came to understand that afternoon is this simple fact: Women do not share their stories enough. Oftentimes, we think that we don't have stories to tell. Or that our stories are not *worthy* enough to tell. The woman's comment made me realize that our stories are important. This revelation was a game-changer.

That one simple sentence led me to coauthor this anthology. Storytelling has been around for thousands of years, but for some reason, as women, we believe our stories are not important. We are taught that telling stories about our successes is bragging. This simply is not true. Men share their stories all the time. They share their successes, they share their gaming wins, and sometimes they even share their defeats. But they learn from each other from these stories, as all people do from the sharing of stories.

In a world where things can be googled and answers can be generated by AI, experience cannot be replaced. It is the sharing of our experiences that will help the next generation. My hope is that by sharing these stories, we will inspire the next generation to forge ahead, discover new industries, work in STEM, advance in male-dominated fields, and contribute their best to society.

This has been an interesting journey. During the course of this book, I approached over 200 women to participate. These women were impressive. They were recognized locally and nationally. These women were speakers, authors, board members, C-suite executives, CEO's, executive directors, and award winners. Of course, this project was not for everyone, but many women told me that they did not believe they had a story to share. These highly successful women were comparing themselves to others or had not yet reached a pinnacle goal that led them to believe their story was not relevant. These are women who have not finished their journeys but have accomplished many things along the way. They did not feel that their accomplishments were *enough*. It was eye-opening.

In a society that still emphasizes unattainable body images, perfectionism, ideal mothers, partners, spouses, leaders, managers, CEOs, and C-Suite executives, we can get swept up in a fairy tale that is not real life. As a recovering perfectionist and control freak, I can tell you that we cannot be good at everything. I have learned to ask for help in the areas where I just am not good at. I am learning to embrace the 80/20 rule. If it is 80% done, then it is finished; the other 20% will work itself out. The truth is, there is no such thing as work/life balance. Sometimes work is important, and sometimes life demands more attention. I think the important thing is not to lose sight of what matters most to you.

In this book, I am proud to share the stories of these women, these *unsung heroines,* who talk about their business successes and failures. The failures are just as important as the successes. Failures are how we learn as humans. The brain is programmed to learn from failure. How these women got around all the "no's," hardships, and life complications to succeed are important stories to share. I want to emphasize that these women were not super women; these women were ordinary women who chose their own paths. They made their journeys one step at a time. Each decision and action that they chose led them to their success today. The choices did not always yield the results they expected, but by choosing and taking action, they gained the knowledge they needed for their next move.

We want to break the cycle where women do not talk about their accomplishments or difficulties. Women need to share so they can help and get help from their colleagues, so that all parties can achieve success. I had many mentors along the way who helped me in my journey. Today, I am a mentor and still a mentee. It is great to be in both positions. Successful people still have coaches and others they surround themselves with to succeed.

We hope you will enjoy the stories we are sharing, and we wish you the best of success on your journey to wherever you want to go. Everyone has a story to share. We are all masterpieces that are still works in progress. Most of your life will be spent on the journey. If you are a lifelong learner, you may never hit the summit. Life will happen whether you want it to or not. Don't miss out on the roller coaster ride by worrying that you are not good enough. Appreciate the ups and downs and trust that you will reach your destination in your own time. And remember to always do two things: share your story and own your masterpiece. It is your work in progress that will bring you joy.

—Debi Corrie
CEO and Founder, Acumaxum, LLC

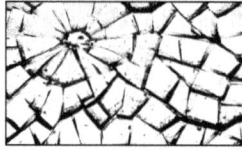

**Debi Corrie**

# Paving New Paths

I did not take the typical route to college. I flunked out my first year, came home from that semester, and realized I still didn't know what I wanted to be when I grew up. My uncertainty led me to decide to work full-time for the next five years while attending night school. I loved math, and accounting seemed like a field that I could enjoy. This was during the 80s, when jobs were really hard to find for accountants. Companies wanted applicants to have experience. By working and going to night school, I could have a significant advantage over other job seekers. When I graduated, I would not only have my degree but also work experience.

With this plan in mind, in 1986, I went on an interview for a little transportation company that specialized in school bus transportation. The company was hiring regional accountants, and I would be helping set up processes and procedures for the area. This was a new position, and I would help create my job. For a 24-year-old, this was a dream come true. I would get to travel all over the United States and learn as I went.

I went to transportation contract locations and documented their billing procedures, rode on buses, and talked to people about what it was like to be a school bus driver. I was learning about the industry and how contracts worked because every contract was different. Then I would come back and write a report.

Other interesting things happened as well. Several managers at these locations, who were men, would tell me unwarranted facts about the industry. For instance, several warned me that transportation had a high divorce rate. A high divorce rate? What on earth did that have to do with my job! Mind you, I never talked about my relationship status with them, yet they were convinced that if I was going to be in this business, I should know the divorce rate. Today, I can look back and laugh at that, realizing they thought they were "protecting me." The reality, though, was much darker: They were pigeonholing me in a hole as a woman.

That incident was hardly the last uncomfortable situation I went through as a woman in this male-dominated position. Imagine being a 24-year-old and telling seasoned managers in their 40s and 50s that they now have to do budgets and then helping them create those budgets. These men were not receptive to change, nor were they receptive to a 24-year-old telling them what they needed to do. Still, I was very stern and forceful. About four weeks into meetings and helping with budgets, my manager called me into his office and said he had been receiving complaints. The complaints were that I was not being nice. His suggestion? That I be nicer. I looked him dead in the eye and said: "How will that work if I'm nice; they will run me over with a 2 by 4?" I continued by expressing that it was hard enough to get them to do what we need them to do, and I had a job to carry out. He asked me what types of objections I had been receiving, and we walked through how to handle them. He taught me to ask more questions when objections were made. Be inquisitive and listen. This made people feel heard and understood. This led to better communication and resolution.

That manager would eventually become a mentor, and he taught me many valuable things. He taught me to speak up for myself and to tell people my goals. The company was growing, and there were many opportunities for growth. I learned to say yes to almost everything. When there was an opportunity to be on the conversion team for a company acquisition, I said yes. When there was an opportunity to start a new contract at a location outside St. Louis, I said yes. When an opportunity for a new corporate job was offered to me, I said yes and left St. Louis to pursue a different path.

Working in the corporate office was a new experience for me. People in the management positions were men; women held mostly clerical jobs and remained absent in C-suite positions. Well, that is not entirely accurate. There was *one* woman supervisor and *one* woman manager. I remember receiving my first review from my manager, who told me my performance was average. I was infuriated. I was actually working extra time to make sure that budgets were completed, variance reports were done, and that managers out in the field understood what we needed so we could make good financial decisions. However, I realized I had not shared these accomplishments with my manager. That experience taught me a valuable lesson: It is important to share your accomplishments and be your own advocate. My manager changed my review, and my pay increased.

A subtle way I knew that I was finally accepted in the industry was by my name. The men in the office called each other by their last names. Everyone in the office called me Debi. A subtle difference, but I noticed. Then one day, I became Robedeau. That day, I knew I had become part of the team.

After working six years in the accounting field, I had no direct reports and told the office that I wanted to work in the field. My first assignment was going to be in the state of Washington. I was single at the time, and the vice president of the area had offered me a contract manager position. I excitedly accepted the position. Since I believed I would be in the state of Washington soon, I had made pretty tough decisions, like turning down my coveted season tickets to the Kansas City Chiefs. About a week later, my new manager called to tell me he was rescinding the offer and giving the position to another manager. He explained that the manager's contract had not been renewed at his school district, and the manager had a family to support. That stung. Don't get me wrong, I have a family. I understand the importance of family, but I had been offered, accepted, and made decisions based on that position. Life was not fair sometimes.

Eventually, a new and better opportunity came along, and I became the area manager for four contracts in southern Illinois. Talk about a great experience. In my first two weeks that summer before school started, the drivers went on strike. Imagine being a new manager, and now you have newspapers calling you about drivers going on strike. We had the news media on site, and I was interviewed on camera. I totally freaked out. I went to my hotel room, called my manager, and frantically said, "I'm out of my depth. What do I do next?" He paused on the other end of the phone and asked, "When does school start?" "It starts in two weeks," I said. He told me, "Go back to the school bus lot, walk outside, and shake each employee's hand and introduce yourself. Get to know them." I took his advice, and it resulted in the drivers coming back to work. The school year started without a hitch.

The experience taught me that everyone is important on the team, from the person who cleans the bathrooms to the bus aides and bus drivers. I remember a mechanic coming to me one time and complaining about "those drivers." It was language that I would not tolerate from the team. I told him that without those drivers, none of us would have a job.

I wanted to create an environment where drivers felt appreciated. When they hit the safety goal for the month, I cooked them pancakes for breakfast. I made myself available, talked to them in the break room, and learned over 100 names and faces. That was a feat for me. I have a hard time with names.

We worked with local school boards, principals, and teachers. It taught me a lot about local government. For the next few years, I ran transportation contracts and transferred to paratransit transportation in 1995. Paratransit was public transportation that operated year-round. During this time, I met another mentor, a woman who had been in the industry for many years. She taught me the ropes of paratransit and helped me get my footing. Working with local government was more difficult than working with local school boards. It gave me more great experience.

I left the industry after 14 years in 2000; by then, I was ready for a change. I could not have asked for a better place to prepare me for the things I would accomplish in the future.

The experience gave me the courage to try new things. I continued to work in male-dominated industries. I worked in insurance and mutual funds for a year. I was the controller at an engineering firm. Then I worked for a large corporation in St Louis, which had only one female in a C-suite position. From there, I moved to a door and hardware company and eventually became their CFO. I worked in so many other industries and in 2020 realized that my experiences could help me start my own company, Acumaxum, a strategic CFO company.

My experience made me an asset to any company as an outsourced CFO. By this time, I had managed IT, handled human resources, completed business acquisitions and sales, worked internationally, dealt with the media, worked with local governments, and had a seat at the table for board meetings. I realized that experience was valuable to small businesses. I began to build a team of CFOs and specifically sought out women and men to be part of the team. It was important to me that we offer flexible work schedules, benefits, and new opportunities to our employees to use their experience to help business owners. Our main focus is to help business owners improve financial performance, cash flow, and make informed business decisions.

When I started my company, I realized women bring a unique perspective to the table for male-run companies. No longer that scared twenty-four-year-old, I understood how valuable my team's advice and experience was to business owners. We are not afraid to speak up and sometimes deliver hard facts. As trusted advisors, we help owners navigate the good times and the challenging times. We are an important advisor at the table, and it is our honor to help these growing businesses succeed.

I have learned so many lessons throughout my career journey. To other aspiring businesswomen who are looking for tips on how to succeed, here are some things to consider:

- Other people and departments are always involved in your decisions. Get their input because it is important to make sure that all the players are involved in a decision that changes policy.

- When you make a mistake, own up to it and offer a solution for correction. Then let your manager or supervisor know how you will handle it in the future and correct the current situation. An apology is not enough; action is needed.

- Being a woman is an advantage. You bring a unique perspective to the boardroom or any room or any C-suite that you belong to. Diverse opinions bring companies to the best solutions and answers. You are part of the solution.

- People will say what people will say. While in transportation, there were slurs made about how I had achieved my success. I ignored them. I knew I worked hard and earned my promotions. You can't let people's bitterness and pettiness get in your way. It is out of your control.

- At some point in your career, you may say yes to too many things, and you need to admit when you're overwhelmed. It happened to me as an overachiever; it'll probably happen to you. Go in and talk to your supervisor or manager, and they will help come up with a solution.

- Don't be afraid to involve the team and ask for help. They want to help you and grow themselves. Remember, we all make mistakes; it is how we learn.

- Make time for the important things: family, friends, pets, neighbors. Time is short; enjoy the roller coaster ride. The highs get us through the lows. Without the lows, we would not know what to appreciate.

- And finally: Share your story! It is the most important thing to do because it will resonate with someone. We are all on a journey together. Your story matters, you matter, share your light. By sharing your light, the next woman will say, "If she can do it, I can do it."

Debi Corrie is a strategist, board member, and public speaker. A proud entrepreneur, she owns four businesses, including Taxpertise, LLP, DJC Media, LLC, SheLEDBass, and Acumaxum, a strategic CFO company. Her firm specializes in helping companies improve cash flow, increase profits, and scale their businesses.

Debi is also the author of *Loving Failure: Getting Control of Your Business Health*. The book focuses on helping business owners understand how to use numbers to build successful companies. She tells stories and gives pointers for new startups and experienced business owners.

Some of Debi's professional achievements include being the recipient of the Gateway to Dreams Impact award, getting recognized by the *St Louis Small Business Monthly* as a Top St. Louis Business Advisor, and becoming a St Louis Titan 100.

In her personal and professional lives, Debi supports women's and children's causes that lift people up.

Please scan the QR code to connect with this author.

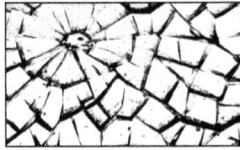

**Kristin Tucker**

# Resilience Through Crisis

"Are you selling or not?"

My business partner, David, had just returned from his vacation, and was asking me this question only a week and a half after Terry, our managing partner and my husband, had passed away. While not surprised by the question, I had hoped I wouldn't hear it quite so soon – or so bluntly.

Just three years earlier, things had seemed much simpler. In early 2001, Terry and David were running out of time for financial success with the software startup they were leading, soon to be a victim of the dotcom bust. I was looking for a new opportunity after nearly twelve years with a locally owned technology consulting company. After many conversations and a lot of planning, we were confident when we launched TDK Technologies (TDK) in April 2001. Life became even more exciting when I learned I was pregnant a few days later.

Our business plan addressed the impact of the economy following the dotcom bust, but there was no way to plan for the impact of 9/11. One of the proudest things I say about TDK is that we're still here, while many more established companies did not survive. The three of us maintained focus on our vision for the company, as Terry and I welcomed our daughter in December 2001, joining his older son and daughter. As we

12

rounded the year into 2002, Terry, David, and I continued driving TDK forward. Then Terry and I got married in July.

No amount of planning could have prepared us for what awaited us in 2003.

Our next challenge started simply enough. One night after a meeting, Terry realized something seemed off with his vision. We weren't terribly concerned, as he'd been warned for years that vision issues could be a side effect of his treatment for rheumatoid arthritis.

Unfortunately, a quick trip to the optometrist uncovered a more serious symptom: his left peripheral vision was impaired in both eyes, revealing that the problem was with the optic nerve. An appointment with a neuro-ophthalmologist led to a CT scan of Terry's brain, which changed everything.

Terry had a brain tumor. Surgery to remove the tumor revealed the worst-case scenario: the tumor was glioblastoma multiforme, the most malignant diagnosis, with a median survival of 15 months.

The next few months were a blur, as I split time between the family, TDK, and learning enough to make informed decisions about treatment for Terry. Ultimately, we found the Tisch Brain Tumor Center at Duke University and the amazing team headed by Dr. Henry Friedman. While we made *lots* of trips between St. Louis and Durham, North Carolina, we were very fortunate that my family stepped in and were wherever they needed to be to take care of our toddler. Terry's ex-wife managed life with the older kids, while David held things together at TDK. My experience in project management became invaluable as I managed the most important project of my life: Terry's treatment.

Terry failed out of Duke's standard treatment plan fairly quickly, which meant learning all I could about clinical trials. Suddenly, our two-day trips every three months became four-day trips every three weeks. (Did

I mention how grateful I am for everyone who managed things at home, providing us with the ability to make those trips?)

The team at Duke referred to Terry as the "poster boy" for the experimental drug trial he was in due to his tremendous response to the treatment.

During this time, Terry, David, and I decided to restructure the ownership of TDK. Given the gravity of Terry's diagnosis, it was the logical thing to do. We moved the controlling interest to me and increased David's share, while keeping a smaller piece in Terry's name. These changes provided for business continuity should the worst happen and gave us the opportunity to have TDK certified as a women-owned business enterprise, a distinction we're proud to hold to this day.

Life was going relatively well on all fronts until Thanksgiving 2003. Terry's treatment was going well; the kids were great. Our son was out of school and working, our older daughter was a freshman at the University of Missouri, and the baby was about to turn two. To top it off, TDK was having its first profitable year. Thanksgiving had always been Terry's favorite holiday, the one day the whole family gathered at our house to eat, laugh, and enjoy time together. His treatment schedule had us at Duke that week, so our family jumped in to cook dinner at our house while we traveled home Thanksgiving morning.

As I wrestled to get luggage, MRI films, a work bag, and my husband through the airport, Terry decided that he was tired of watching me juggle everything on every trip. He picked up our large suitcase, resulting in an audible "POP" and a look of agony on his face. It wasn't easy, but we were able to get home and enjoy the holiday with our family. A trip to his doctor the next day revealed what the doctor believed was the source of the pain.

An MRI showed a couple of minor herniations, so the doctor suggested Terry see a chiropractor. The pain persisted despite several adjustments, transforming daily tasks into major challenges and pulling his focus away from treatment for the brain tumor. Further tests, including bone density, returned normal results, leaving doctors baffled. We didn't understand the extent to which his back pain impacted his treatment until another trip to Duke in early 2004.

The travel itself for that trip was more difficult because of Terry's reduced mobility. At his appointment, we learned that the amazing response he'd been having to the trial drugs had ended. He'd no longer continue in the trial, but we'd meet with the team again the next day to determine the next treatment protocol. Obviously disappointed in the news, we headed back to the hotel so he could take a nap, and I could catch up on some work.

When I woke Terry a couple of hours later, we shared in the terrifying realization that he couldn't get out of bed. I called 911, and EMS techs moved him out of the hotel to the hospital. After a series of tests, one of the doctors from the Brain Tumor Center team clipped the most perplexing X-rays I'd seen onto the light board in the room. Having seen a lot of film at this point (more than a year into his diagnosis), I looked but saw only shadows, instead of the clearly defined bones I would have expected. The doctor explained that I was looking at severe drug-induced osteoporosis (the shadows were Terry's vertebrae). By his count, Terry had seven compression fractures in his spine.

After a complicated flight home, we met with a spine specialist to discuss corrective surgery, which was actually two surgeries. Seven fractures were too many to correct at once. Once again, I was grateful for my project management skills. I used every skill I had to coordinate two surgeries between chemotherapy cycles while managing the timing of medications to prevent the blood-clotting side effect of his treatments. After the successful repair of his spine, Terry entered a skilled nursing facility for extensive physical therapy to rebuild his strength for the fight ahead.

Primary brain tumors are tricky things. They're considered "smart" because they are comprised of nervous system cells, and can mutate to protect themselves from treatment designed to destroy them. A limited number of treatment options can penetrate the blood-brain barrier. In many cases, those treatments can be as lethal as the tumor itself.

Ultimately, brain surgery, radiation therapy, more than a year of chemotherapy, blood clots, two back surgeries, and a string of infections proved too much for Terry. We lost him to sepsis on July 20, 2004, two days after our second wedding anniversary.

In the days that followed Terry's death, I made sure David went on his family vacation (even threatening to have Terry haunt him!). Then, I searched for any opportunity to be productive. I worked with TDK's benefits broker to remove Terry from our renewal calculation. This second pass through underwriting changed the price tag dramatically, from a 25 percent increase to no increase, an astronomical shift in expense for a fledgling small business.

While that conversation about what I planned to do with the company after Terry's death started a little rough with David's blunt, "Are you selling or not?", he and I found common ground and pretty quickly figured out what this new two-person partnership would look like. We renewed our joint commitment to TDK – and what a journey it's been.

Ever since, David and I have joked that Terry got back to work in August 2004, as the business took off. TDK grew 75 percent in 2005 over 2004 and averaged 50 percent growth year-over-year from 2004 to 2008. We've received a variety of recognitions over the years, but more importantly, we've employed hundreds of team members and provided quality software development services to our clients since April 2001.

Celebrating 24 years in business is a little surreal, and at the same time, I couldn't be prouder. While we continue to thrive, hurdles have appeared along the way. But the personal and professional challenges of Terry's illness and loss revealed unknown resilience and support. Now I know I can survive and thrive after any nose-dive.

Early in my career, I never would have imagined founding a company or becoming a widow at 36. If I could give a piece of advice to my younger self, it would be to always trust your gut and know that your family and friends will always be there to support you when the weight of the world seems too much. It can be difficult to believe in yourself and go with your gut, particularly if it goes against the grain of what others are telling you. There will certainly be times when it doesn't pan out, but more often than not, it will take you where you're meant to be.

Kristin Tucker is co-founder and managing principal of TDK Technologies, LLC, a technology consulting firm specializing in custom software development, based in Chesterfield, Missouri. She was included on the *St. Louis Business Journal's* Most Influential Business Women list in 2013 and is a member of the St. Louis Titan Hall of Fame. Kristin serves on the Aquinas Institute board of trustees and as a member of the planning committee for Gateway to Innovation, the largest technology conference in the Midwest.

Outside of work, Kristin is the proud mom of three and even prouder "Gigi" to her seven grandchildren. She enjoys spending time with family and friends, traveling, attending concerts, and watching St. Louis City SC, the St. Louis Blues, and Ole Miss football. Kristin lives in Chesterfield, Missouri, with her youngest daughter. In the summer, you can find her on her boat at the Lake of the Ozarks.

Please scan the QR code to connect with this author.

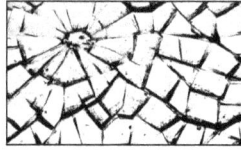

**Bing Dempewolf**

# The Invisible Backbone of Every Great Company

If business strategies were blueprints, human resources (HR) would be the foundation—rarely admired but absolutely essential. While CEOs celebrate record quarters and marketers win awards for flashy campaigns, HR professionals work in the quiet spaces between the headlines, ensuring the organization doesn't crumble beneath its own growth. We are the silent architects who build the scaffolding that holds up the entire enterprise, the invisible hands that steady the ladder while others climb to applause.

I've spent my career as one of these silent architects—first as an HR executive navigating corporate conundrums, then as the founder of TAI-CHI Consulting, where I've made it my mission to prove that people strategy isn't just a support function, but the very bedrock of business success.

My journey has taught me this undeniable truth: The most brilliant business plan will fail without an equally brilliant people plan. A company can have groundbreaking products, visionary leadership, and endless capital, but without the right people systems in place, it will eventually collapse under the weight of its own dysfunction.

Yet here's the painful irony: While organizations invest millions in management consultants to design their future and hire celebrity CEOs to lead them there, they routinely treat HR as an administrative after-thought—until disaster strikes. It's only when the discrimination lawsuit hits, when the toxic culture drives away top talent, or when the failed merger reveals deep cultural rifts that executives suddenly remember HR exists. By then, it's often too late.

This is my story—not as a celebrity CEO gracing magazine covers, but as an unsung conductor who has learned that real leadership isn't about taking bows. It's about ensuring the entire organizational orchestra plays in perfect harmony, even when no one in the audience realizes who's keeping time. It's about doing the hard, often invisible work of:

- Building systems that allow talent to flourish
- Safeguarding culture before toxicity takes root
- Anticipating people risks long before they become crises
- Creating conditions or success that feel effortless to those who benefit from them

The greatest compliment I ever received came from a CEO who said, "Things just seem to work better when you're involved. I can't quite put my finger on why." That's the essence of strategic HR at its best: You know it's working when everything feels seamless, problems are solved before they escalate, and the organization thrives without anyone quite realizing how much work went into making it happen.

This is the paradox we navigate every day: Our greatest successes are invisible by design. When we do our jobs perfectly, no one notices. But when we fail—or when leadership ignores our warnings—the conse-quences are front-page news.

Over my four decades in this field, I've learned that being the invis-ible backbone isn't a weakness—it's a superpower. It allows us to operate under the radar and make change happen without triggering resistance. It enables us to see the truth that others miss because we're not caught up in office politics. All of this allows us to build lasting solutions rather than chasing quick fixes that look good on paper.

The companies that understand this—that recognize HR as a strategic partner rather than a support function—are the ones that weather storms, attract top talent, and sustain success over decades. The others? They eventually learn the hard way that no business can outperform its people systems.

This chapter is an invitation to see what happens behind the curtain—to understand how the silent architects of business actually operate, and why their work matters more than ever in today's volatile world. It's also a challenge: What could your organization achieve if you stopped treating HR as an afterthought and started recognizing it as the foundation it truly is?

The future belongs to companies that understand one simple truth: Your business strategy is only as strong as the people strategy supporting it. Everything else is just noise.

## The Accidental HR Revolutionary

I never set out to be an HR executive. Like many women in business, I stumbled into this career—first out of necessity, then out of passion. My awakening came early at a manufacturing firm where 40% annual turnover was considered "just part of the business."

I calculated the true cost of turnover, which amounted to $2.3 million annually in recruitment and lost productivity. Determined to make a change, I redesigned shift schedules, reducing attrition by 58% in just 18 months. Through this experience, I proved that "soft" HR changes could drive "hard" business results.

HR isn't about policies—it's about understanding why people break them.

Years later, I sat in an executive meeting where the CEO announced plans to expand into three new markets. The room erupted in applause until someone asked, "Who will lead these new teams? How will we recruit 200 specialized roles? What's the plan to maintain our culture across time zones?" Silence hit and flooded the room. Eventually, the CFO shrugged and replied: "That's HR's problem."

That moment crystallized my life's work and philosophy that HR must be at the strategy table from day one, not brought in after the decisions are made.

Corporate America often treats HR like an emergency response team—only summoned when workplace fires are already raging. But after forty years in the trenches, I've learned our real value lies not in putting out fires, but in preventing the spark. My "Fixer's Toolkit" represents the invisible infrastructure that keeps organizations from combusting, built on one radical premise: the best HR work happens when no one notices it's happening.

Take lawsuit prevention, where most assume we exist to process complaints or terminate employees. The truth? Our greatest victories occur in the quiet moments before attorneys get involved. I'll never forget the senior director who dismissed my sensitivity training invitation with, *"I don't need to be taught how to talk to people.* Six months later, his "offhand joke" at a team happy hour triggered a $250,000 discrimination settlement. This predictable tragedy inspired our three-pronged defense: neuroscience-based microaggression workshops that rewired managerial blind spots, anonymous "Culture Thermometer" surveys mapping departmental trust levels in real time, and our "Stoplight" reporting system allowing discreet concern escalation. The payoff? A 68% drop in formal complaints, and teams that rediscovered how to collaborate without collateral damage.

The same preventative philosophy applies to cultural toxicity, a corporate cancer that's curable when caught early but fatal at metastasis.

Most leaders miss the vital signs: the subtle eyerolls when certain names arise in meetings, the star contributor who retreats into monosyllabic responses, or the team that armor-plates every email with unnecessary CCs. These aren't personality quirks. They're the organizational equivalent of a fever, and by the time the thermometer reads "danger," the infection has often spread beyond containment. The fixer's role? To be the cultural oncologist who spots abnormal cells before they turn malignant.

In a hyper-growth company where 38% annual turnover was casually dismissed as "industry standard," our exit interviews uncovered a disturbing pattern—82% of departing employees cited one particular VP's toxic "my way or the highway" leadership style. When we presented these findings to the CEO, the response was telling: "*I don't care if he's difficult, he gets results.*" So, we launched a stealth intervention. First, we implemented 360° feedback disguised as "Leadership Accelerator Programs" to avoid triggering defensiveness. Then we waged data warfare, revealing the VP's true cost: his teams took triple the sick days and produced 40% fewer innovations. Within twelve months, we retained 73% of at-risk talent, and remarkably, the VP improved his own leadership scores. The lesson? Lasting change happens when you give people tools instead of ultimatums.

The chasm between administrative and strategic HR becomes clearest in talent management. One reacts to vacancies while the other prevents them. This truth hit hard when an organization rejected my 18-month talent mapping proposal as "HR overcomplicating hiring." Their $1.2 million wake-up call came when their linchpin employee resigned, forcing them to pay a recruiter 30% of a $400,000 salary, bleed $15,000 daily in delayed product launches, and ultimately settle for a mismatched hire who departed within six months. Our strategic alternative involved

23

creating "Skills Gap Heat Maps" aligned with product roadmaps, identifying three internal candidates for succession development, and establishing "Knowledge Transfer Protocols" for mission-critical roles. The takeaway? Reactive hiring remains corporate America's most overlooked cost center, while organizations treating talent acquisition as a strategic discipline save millions—and preserve their sanity.

The true power of strategic HR lies in its invisibility. Our greatest triumphs are the disasters we prevent before they ever see daylight. While sales teams toast to new clients and engineers celebrate product launches, our victories whisper in the negative space: the discrimination lawsuit that never materialized, the star performer who nearly left but chose to stay, the acquisition that integrated seamlessly without cultural casualties. Herein lies the open secret of exceptional HR leadership—when your work goes unnoticed, you've succeeded. Our mission isn't to chase recognition, but to architect environments where people thrive, unaware of the deliberate design holding everything together. This is the beautiful contradiction of our role: We quantify our impact in absences—the conflicts that never escalated, the turnover that never happened, the crises that never erupted. And if we've executed flawlessly? We leave no trace behind, just organizations that hum along effortlessly, never realizing how intentionally their foundation was built.

Early in my career, I resented working in the shadows. Then a mentor reframed it: *"Bing, do surgeons need applause for successful operations? No—the patient's health is the reward. Your patients are companies."*

This mindset shift allowed me to do several things. It taught me to leverage stealth influence (coaching resistant CEOs through "their" epiphanies), avoid political landmines (when HR isn't seen as a threat, leaders listen more), and focus on sustainable impact (not chasing trendy initiatives that look good on LinkedIn).

The flip side? Being undervalued has catastrophic consequences. For example, in one case study, a manufacturer ignored our frontline burnout warnings. The result? A $14 million unionization campaign. In another example, a startup dismissed our hiring timeline projections. They missed their product launch by five months, losing first-mover advantage to a competitor. The lesson? Companies that treat HR as trivial eventually pay, often in ways that make headlines.

## TAI-CHI Consulting

TAI-CHI Consulting entered the market without fanfare—no press releases, just a single former employer turned client who had witnessed my work's transformative power. Our value proposition was radical in its simplicity: We solved the problems companies didn't know they had. Through Pre-Strategy People Audits, we once prevented a $50M expansion disaster by exposing nonexistent talent pipelines. Our Culture CPR methodology resuscitated toxic teams before they crashed company morale. Most powerfully, our Stealth Equity Overhauls corrected pay disparities without triggering executive egos. The magic was in the framing. CEOs would never admit they needed "HR help," but they eagerly invested in "strategic workforce optimization."

The path from invisible operator to strategic partner begins with translation: converting "soft" HR concepts into the hard language of business. Engagement becomes productivity metrics, and culture morphs into customer satisfaction drivers. Success lies in building quiet alliances: partnering with CFOs on workforce ROI models, equipping sales teams with retention data for client negotiations. When claiming credit, the approach matters. Not "Look what I did!" but "When we implemented X, it drove Y outcome—let's scale this."

To all the other businesswomen who are in the HR industry, I say to you: **Command your presence—don't request it.** Stop bringing "people problems" to the C-suite. Bring them business solutions wrapped in data, dollars, and decisive impact. I didn't ask for a seat. I showed them the cost of not having me in the room: the turnover bleeding millions, the innovation lost to disengagement, the legal time bombs hidden in toxic cultures. Speak the language of power—profit and risk—with unwavering clarity. Quantify your intuition. Validate your insight with numbers that silence doubt. Your influence doesn't start when you're invited; it starts when you demonstrate that every strategic goal depends on the systems you build and the talent you protect. Don't seek validation—deliver value so undeniable that leadership leans in when you speak, not because they have to, but because they can't afford not to. You aren't a function—you're a force. Now go make them see it.

Bing Dempewolf is the founder and CEO of TAI-CHI Consulting, a people-focused human resources and culture transformation firm. With more than 35 years in HR leadership across industries, Bing has built a reputation for helping organizations create inclusive, resilient, and high-performing workplaces.

She understands the challenges leaders face in finding, hiring, motivating, managing, and retaining good employees. Her ability to communicate effectively across all levels of an organization develops instant credibility and trust among employees.

In addition to leading TAI-CHI Consulting, Bing serves as the chief operating officer of Mental Health Code, a company dedicated to advancing mental health awareness, education, and community support. She also is an accomplished author and serves on multiple boards, where she shares her expertise in leadership and community impact.

Driven by her belief that business can be both strategic and compassionate, Bing empowers leaders to align culture with strategy and unlock their people's full potential.

Please scan the QR code to connect with this author.

**Kristene Rosser**

# A Real Estate Adventure

After a few auditor jobs and a nasty divorce, I decided to re-enter real estate! I got my license back in 2001 and then immediately decided to go back to college for my master's degree in accounting. In 2011, I decided I needed a change and pulled my real estate license out of referral. I started with a big firm, opened a branch office for a small local organization, and decided I could do way better on my own. I learned how to work the job and learned even more about how *not* to do the job. In 2018, I decided to take the leap and open my own real estate brokerage—KRS Realty, LLC. I was ready to build something of my own. Plus, I had this vision of a team that's happy, productive, and—fingers crossed—making money.

The struggles hit fast. First up: licensing. I had my real estate license, sure, but setting up a brokerage meant jumping through hoops with the state. Paperwork, fees, and a million little rules I didn't know existed, like companywide standard operating procedures (SOP), state law requirements, and errors-and-omissions insurance. I spent hours on hold with the licensing board, trying to sound like I knew what I was doing while internally freaking out. Money was already flying out the door, and I hadn't even secured an office yet.

Up next on the list of growing challenges was finding a space. I wanted something that screamed "We're legit!" but didn't cost my life savings.

After weeks of scouring listings (ironic, right?), I found a cozy office in a quiet executive park and a landlord who didn't seem like he'd nickel-and-dime me. It was a basement unit tucked far off the beaten path, enough room for a few desks, and a vibe that said, "We sell houses, and we are a warm and friendly family." I signed the lease, feeling like a boss, only to realize I now had to furnish the place, hire a team, and, oh yeah, figure out how to actually run a brokerage.

Then came the team. I wanted KRS Realty, LLC to be different—none of that cutthroat, every-agent-for-themselves nonsense. I envisioned a crew that supported each other, shared leads, and actually enjoyed coming to work. Finding those people, though? Not easy. I interviewed a dozen agents, some of whom acted like they were auditioning for some strange real estate reality show called "Who Can Sell the Most Mansions?" I finally hired two: They were a duo that I used to work with at the big brokerage, and they were looking for more flexibility and a way to grow their business unrestrictedly! I was so blessed they decided to come over and give our little start-up a try.

Our first month was a disaster. We had two listings, one client who ghosted us after a showing, and our pipeline was barely existent. I was burning through cash on rent, utilities, and bakery runs to keep morale up. The duo had a great system in place; however, they were still trying to get all their leads and marketing switched over. That is harder than you think. I hired an administrative assistant who kept pulling me away from selling because we had to create the office procedures and prepare for the entry audit that we knew would come in the first six months. My son got his license and came on board with no clue how to do anything! I immediately had to put on my instructor hat and help him navigate the job.

The low point came when I realized we'd spent $5,500 on furnishings for the office to "impress clients," but we hadn't had a single client walk through the door. I was lying awake at night, wondering if I'd made a huge mistake, when I turned on my computer to check our internal software and saw that one of my agents had turned in their first sale. It was an investment portfolio worth upwards of $1 million. Finally, we were on the map. I didn't sleep that night, but for a good reason this time.

That portfolio sale was our first win. We were on the map, netting us a decent commission and some buzz. Agents who kept a daily look at production and sales were finally noticing us, and we gained traction and visibility. We started working on video tours of homes and virtual open houses. Then we offered staging services as a marketing strategy included in our fees. People loved it. Pretty soon, we were getting calls from sellers who'd seen our videos, and suddenly, we had listings—modest ones, but listings, nonetheless. We realized staging and video were our ticket to breaking through.

But success brought new problems. With more listings came more work, and our little team was stretched to the limit. My administrative assistant was taking work home, and she really needed to take a day off. I was doing everything—answering phones, scheduling showings, handling paperwork, and trying to keep everyone motivated. I hadn't taken a day off in months, and I was starting to snap at people over dumb stuff. My son pulled me aside one day and said, "You're gonna burn out, and then we're all screwed." This pulled me back into reality. I decided to create boundaries and discipline to ensure my schedule accommodated me twice a week. I also asked each agent to ensure they were scheduling a day off each week to focus on their family and themselves.

By month six, things were clicking. We closed five deals in one month, all single-family homes. The commission checks started rolling in, and I could finally pay myself without wincing. The team was in better spirits, too. The agents and our admin found a groove, and we were able to put processes in place that worked for everyone. We even had a team happy hour where nobody complained about work—a miracle.

However, we all knew that day was approaching. The day that could easily undo or at least significantly stall our momentum. The dreaded "Open Your Office, the State Audits You" audit. Fortunately, we had all our processes in place, and we passed with flying colors! Thank goodness for procedures and a detail-oriented admin. Details are not my thing!

By the end of our first year, KRS Realty was profitable. Not "buy a yacht" profitable, but enough to pay the bills, give the team bonuses, and start planning for growth. We had active listings, amazing buyer clients, a steady stream of leads, and a reputation as the no-nonsense, friendly brokerage in town. Clients loved our vibe—professional but not stuffy, with agents who actually cared about finding them the right home. The office was buzzing with energy, and I started hearing my team laugh more than they complained, which felt like a win in itself.

Looking back, the struggles were worth it. The sleepless nights, the empty bank account, the moments I doubted myself—they all led to something real. KRS Realty wasn't just a business; it was a place where agents could grow their business easily. We could share strategies and not feel like we were getting stabbed in the back. Here, learning happened without hesitation, and our admin could keep us all sane by taking care of our paperwork so we could go out and sell more property. We were a team, and we were making it work.

Now, in 2025, we're a smaller group, but we still have the same outlook and culture. We put our clients first. We take pride in keeping real estate simple, drama-free, and we ensure everyone is taken care of like family. Looking back, I wish I had started my business before 2018. Even through the global pandemic, we thrived as a group. We kept each other positive, and we lifted our clients up to ensure they were safe and happy with their next forever home. It is a great feeling handing someone keys to their first house. I hope everyone gets to experience that for themselves one day. It definitely doesn't get old.

When you catch yourself lying awake at night, second-guessing your choice to start your own company, you're not alone—every woman who's built something from scratch has been there. Those sleepless moments are just your brain wrestling with the big leap you took, and that's okay. Remind yourself why you started: that spark of an idea, the freedom to call the shots, or the chance to make a real impact. Focus on the wins, no matter how small—a happy customer, a killer pitch, or even just surviving a tough week. Build a support network of other entrepreneurs who get it; their stories and advice will ground you. Take it one step at a time, and trust that your courage got you this far. You're tougher than the toughest doubts.

Hope comes from knowing you're not just building a business; you're carving out a legacy. Every late night, every hurdle you clear, is proof you're creating something meaningful that can inspire others. Keep a journal of your progress to see how far you've come when the doubts creep in. Connect with mentors or join communities where women lift each other up. Those connections are gold. And don't underestimate the power of a quick walk or a good laugh to reset your mindset. You're not just chasing a dream; you're showing other women what's possible. Keep going, because every step forward is a win for you and everyone watching.

Kristene Rosser is the owner of KRS Realty, LLC, and a partner of Taxpertise, LLP. She earned her BSA and MSA from Southern Illinois University Edwardsville and spent four years as a civilian auditing the U.S. Army. Two of those years were served in Iraq under Operation Iraqi Freedom and Operation New Dawn. In April 2018, she launched KRS Realty, LLC as the Designated Managing Broker/Owner with a mission of keeping real estate simple.

Kristene helped found Taxpertise, LLP in 2012 to support individuals and companies through their annual income tax journeys. Over the last eighteen years, she has volunteered as a Boy Scout leader. During that time, she trained numerous scouts and adults in leadership principles, serving on Wood Badge, Kodiak, and NYLT staff, and helping over twenty young men and one young woman earn the rank of Eagle Scout.

Please scan the QR code to connect with this author.

**Beth Gunter**

# When the Ground Shifts, So Do I

From my earliest childhood, my parents instilled principles of salesmanship in me. I learned how to negotiate, how to present value, and how to persevere. So, imagine my shock when, after years of building my career, I found myself displaced not once, not twice, but three times in the span of a few years.

The back-to-back career blows felt like a sucker punch. The wind escaped my lungs, and I struggled to process the reality. A million questions raced through my mind: *Why? What did I do wrong? How would I support my family? Pregnant and over forty, who would hire me? How would I secure health insurance? How could I even tell my family without feeling like a failure?* The uncertainty surged through me and crushed me in an avalanche of doubt.

The mental battle continued and expanded relentlessly. Shame whispered that I wasn't good enough. Fear told me I'd never recover. But then something else stirred within me—beyond doubt, shame, and fear—anger. How dare those key stakeholders, the ones who chose to let me go without warning or explanation, make me doubt myself? How dare the timing, the economy, the weight of being pregnant and over forty, conspire to try and break me? I had fought too hard for everything I had, and I wasn't about to let setbacks rewrite my story.

Throughout my career, I have faced skepticism. People told me I couldn't grow into leadership, that I'd never get promoted, that I couldn't drive real change within an organization. They doubted my ability to earn, to influence, or to win on behalf of a client. But each time, those doubts became fuel for my forward momentum. Repeatedly, I proved the naysayers wrong—and this time would be no different.

After each punch to the gut, I curled around the pain and allowed myself to grieve briefly. I cried. I felt the sting of disappointment. And then, I rose from the mat and stood again in the center of the ring, gloves raised. I spoke with my family, created a game plan for the type of company I was looking to work for, identified the more intangible characteristics that would make me happy long term, and lastly, what my ideal role would entail.

The next day, I picked up the phone and started networking with renewed urgency and intensity. I reached out to former colleagues I hadn't spoken to in years, followed every lead, sent personalized messages late into the night, and scheduled back-to-back virtual and in-person coffee chats with anyone willing to talk with me. I researched companies, tailored every resume and cover letter, and showed up to every conversation prepared, not just with my pitch but with curiosity and determination. Rejection still stung, but I reminded myself of advice from a former boss: "I'll give you today to have your pity party. But tomorrow, you shake it off and get back to work." That advice became my guiding principle: Feel it, process the disappointment, embrace it, and then let it go. Don't let it define you.

## The Unexpected Journey

Back then, I didn't see myself as an entrepreneur or a business leader. So, in college, I majored in English, drawn to the written word, the dependability of grammar rules, the rhythm of poetry, and the intimacy of stories, not the cold logic of balance sheets. My business acumen in college was limited to lessons from retail and leasing management. I barely knew how to balance a checkbook, let alone run a business. But even then, the seeds were there. I had a natural pull toward leadership—unhoned, untapped, and invisible to me at the time, though not to others. While I doubted my place at the head of any table, those around me quietly took note of my instincts, my drive, and my ability to rally others. Eventually, life decided to write my business plan for me.

After college, I landed in the car industry, a world I knew absolutely nothing about. On my first day, I was handed a ring of keys and asked to "bring around" a vehicle. Simple enough . . . until I realized I couldn't tell a Dodge Stratus from a Neon or Intrepid. I had to walk behind each car, reading the make and model off the back, as if I were cramming for a pop quiz, just to match them to the keys. And just when I thought I had it figured out, I proudly opened a car door, slid into the driver's seat, only to discover it wasn't part of our fleet at all. It was someone's *personal* vehicle. Welcome to the car business. But beneath the embarrassment and steep learning curve, I started to understand something important: Success wasn't about knowing engines or trim packages, it was about connection. Relationships. Trust. That revelation led me into B2B sales, where I discovered my true "magic sauce" for success: authenticity, consistency, and strategy. Selling wasn't about being the loudest in the room; it was about being the most trusted.

Suddenly, all those childhood lessons in negotiation, expressing value, and perseverance snapped into focus. Growing up, I constantly pitched my parents, justifying every dollar for debate team events, field trips, or new clothes. At some point, selling stopped feeling like a career decision and revealed itself for what it truly was: second nature.

## Breaking Barriers

The road to success in sales challenges everyone and is especially difficult for a woman navigating any male-dominated industry. Early in my career, I learned that perception mattered. In the South, I wore skirts to sales meetings, not for fashion, but to ensure I was heard. As the first female leader in my company to have a baby, I concealed my pregnancy until I was in my ninth month, not out of shame but because I understood the biases.

My career took me across several industries—automobiles, financial services, consulting, EdTech, publishing, and finally, technology. Reinvention became my specialty.

And then, the global pandemic entered from stage left and became an unwelcome and disruptive part of our world. "Stay home" orders forced me to pivot yet again, proving, especially to myself, that I could adapt and thrive in any environment.

## The Displacement Struggle

Losing a job is more than just losing a paycheck; it's losing stability, routine, and, in many ways, identity. The three gut punches in a few years piled loss upon loss. The first shattered me. It made me question everything about my career and self-worth. The second, just two years into my new security, terrified me. My quickly rebuilt security vanished. The third punch, within another two years, infuriated me. This last time was a little different; I was pregnant, vulnerable, and uninsured. The financial hit was brutal.

The common thread each time? I refused to stay down. I leaned on my mantras:

- **"Everything happens for a reason."** Even when I lose faith, I hold onto the hope of something better.

- **"Look for the silver lining."** Every setback carries a lesson.

- **"Job searching is a full-time job."** Show up for myself and my future.

My family's witness to how I responded to everything produced additional motivation. My resilience, or lack of it, carried lessons for how to face these challenges. So, I continued to dust myself off and keep moving forward.

## A Servant Heart and the Power of Giving Back

My involvement with St. Louis Children's Hospital shines among my greatest strengths during the toughest times. In my volunteer work there, I found purpose, validation, and a reminder of what truly matters. A servant heart allows me to keep my wits during life's difficult seasons and ensures that I continue to show up, not just for myself but for my community.

After life-saving care for my youngest child, I cannot pay it forward enough to this amazing medical support team. Our four-and-a-half-month experience in the NICU has kept life's rough patches in perspective. When I walk into the hospital, when I see the children and families fighting battles much bigger than my own, I am reminded of the resilience of the human spirit. My setbacks suddenly feel surmountable, and I am filled with gratitude for the opportunity to serve.

## Networking: My Superpower

The key to my comeback, my rising from the mat after that third punch to the gut? My network picked me up and kept me standing. Every new opportunity resulted from business relationships nurtured over time. Networking transforms the pursuit of job leads into genuine connections to colleagues who provide support and guidance during those difficult times.

As I rebuilt my career, I sought opportunities to "give back" even more. That desire led to the creation of the **One Degree of Separation**

**Networking** event. What began as a small gathering blossomed into a thriving community. Even during the pandemic, we found ways to keep the momentum alive. Seven, almost eight, years later, this semi-quarterly event continues to bring professionals together, proving that when we lift each other off the mat after a knock-out punch, we create incredible results.

## Gravitas in Leadership

One defining moment in my journey of resilience and transformation was an executive women's leadership course that taught the importance of **gravitas**, the presence and confidence that command respect. Women are often expected to downplay their achievements. But I had worked too hard to be invisible.

Recently, I was invited to mentor for a second consecutive year for the *Business Journal*; this year was focused on networking and how to help women network for results. When I shared the news on LinkedIn, a lifelong friend of my father forwarded it to him. My dad and my stepmom (also affectionately referred to as my "bonus" mom), Nina Totenberg, both people who I have admired in various ways all my life, reached out to say how proud they were—not just of my career, but of the mother, wife, and leader I had become. It was a reminder that, while external validation isn't everything, it can be deeply meaningful.

Now, I mentor and coach the next generation of women leaders, encouraging them to embrace their uniqueness and never shrink themselves for anyone. Leadership isn't about fitting into someone else's mold. Creating your own mold, now, that's gravitas.

## The Unsung Heroine

Women in business are all unsung heroines. We often work twice as hard for half the recognition. But I do it anyway, because I believe in what I'm building. Through every challenge, every reinvention, and every triumph, I've realized that my other superpower is resilience.

My message to every aspiring woman in business is this: You don't need permission to sing your own song or follow your own beat. You don't need to hit every pitch perfectly or hear a chorus of praise. Enlist your network as fuel for both your resilience and the confidence to know you belong. Like every heroine who chooses her own path, summon your courage, find your voice, and speak with the power only you possess. Because you do.

Beth Gunter is chief revenue officer and partner at Spry Digital. Her strategic sales philosophies have transformed the agency's approach to client relationships and fueled a record-breaking revenue increase since 2022. Under her leadership, Spry has earned industry recognition for both growth and digital excellence. With over two decades of executive experience, Beth has led global business development for Fortune 500 companies, earning national awards and spearheading high-impact partnerships. She is a two-time international best-selling author and a 2024 honoree of both *The Top 50 Women Leaders of Missouri and St. Louis* and *The Top 50 Women Chief Revenue Officers*. Beyond business, Beth serves as chairperson of the St. Louis Children's Hospital Development Board and mentors emerging leaders through *Mentoring Monday*. A mother of four, devoted wife, and passionate photographer, she finds joy in travel, gardening, and family dance parties—infusing every part of her life with creativity, empathy, and ambition

Please scan the QR code to connect with this author.

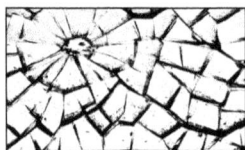

**Shea Peffly**

# Entrepreneur by Accident

Most kids right out of high school have no idea what they want to do with their lives. Isn't it a bit unrealistic and unfair to expect them to? How can they really have a clear map guiding them toward their destination when they have so little experience? At 18, I certainly did not have a clear plan for my life, particularly my career, but I found out very quickly what I did *not* want to do, which ended up being just as helpful. Like most young people, my first job was working in the food industry.

I worked at Gridley's Fine Bar-B-Q, which was a privately owned barbecue restaurant in Memphis, Tennessee. Now, "Fine" might have applied to the customer experience, and *maybe* the food, but certainly not to how I smelled every day, leaving each shift. I reeked of BBQ and can't believe I can still eat it today. I then worked at a grocery store as a checker. This job saw me through college, but I still had no idea what career I wanted long-term.

After graduating from college, I got a job as a telemarketer. Except this job was not much better. Yes, I finally did not have to do a complete scrub down to rid myself of a barbecue odor when I got home from a shift, but I was still in a place of disillusionment. It proved to be just as monotonous as my other jobs, as I spent my days stuck on the phone. While this job was by no means a great one, it nevertheless gave me a clearer picture of what I *did* want in a career. And that was autonomy. And some degree of decision-making. And, above all, a sense of purpose and the knowledge that I was making an impact. Now, I had no idea what industry was the best fit for me, but I knew that I needed three things.

At this young age, did I envision becoming an entrepreneur and owning my own business? Of course not! And yet, that is where my various jobs, experiences, and personality have led me. I'm definitely an entrepreneur by accident, not by intention, because I didn't know I was an entrepreneur at the time of even going down this path. I'm not like the typical entrepreneurs you hear about who "always knew" this road was for them. I was never that precocious seven-year-old building a lemonade stand and eagerly advertising it to neighbors. Nor was I that eager girl scout relentlessly getting one more person to buy cookies in order to meet her quota. In fact, when I was young, I did not particularly enjoy being in the spotlight. It would have been enough out of my comfort zone to even initiate the conversations needed to talk to people, let alone to begin an entrepreneurial journey!

I have come to this place as an independent businesswoman by saying yes to paths that my heart has led me to in the moment. These paths have been far from clear and straightforward, but they have nevertheless allowed me to hone in and discover my real passion and purpose. While the path was full of complete chaos for a while, it eventually calmed down, and I thankfully arrived at my destination—a stable place where I have a successful career that allows me to maintain autonomy, have the flexibility of managing my own schedule, and follow my passion for helping others.

In most cases, when we hear of entrepreneurs, we hear of the incredible success stories that seem to magically happen overnight. These scenarios do exist, but they are not the norm. Any business owner creating their own company can tell you the brutal reality: that success does not happen overnight. It takes years to establish your business and obtain consistent profitability.

I ended up in the business consulting industry purely through trial and error. After years of working for various people, I accidentally discovered that I wouldn't mind owning a business, but I had not figured out the best industry for me. I first ventured into entrepreneurship part-time in 2005, when my husband and I owned a recording studio—very different from business consulting. I did it part-time because I am a risk-taker at times, but not that kind of risk-taker! I did not feel comfortable throwing caution to the wind and quitting my other company yet. For several years, I continued this format of working for other companies while also feeding my entrepreneurial bug. This approach worked for me as it felt more stable than jumping into the entrepreneur waters without a safety jacket.

When we owned our recording studios, we helped artists be the best at their craft. This need to help others succeed and be the best version of themselves is something that I kept up, no matter what industry I was in. I worked in construction for 14 years and worked with veterans' benefits for 12 years. As the daughter of a Marine sergeant, working with veterans was certainly a cause that was close to my heart. While I have owned various industries, the common thread that binds and connects everything is having that commitment to helping others. It took me a while to discover that helping others in consulting projects is my special niche. I have helped many people in my journey and career. All in different paths, and it has transformed me into who I am today.

Even while I was working part-time as an entrepreneur and enjoying the newfound freedom that came with that role, it had its difficulties. At that time, my kids were at home and in school. Finding that balance between being a good business owner and a fully present mom was quite challenging. I wanted to exhibit quality in both roles and not let anything slip on either side. Not surprisingly, I had good and bad days. There were moments when I went crying to my husband or another close confidante and told them that I wanted to quit because it was too hard. It was just too much, and I had bitten off more than I could handle. However, after having these breakdowns and receiving the reassurance from my loved ones that I did have what it took to succeed, the tears running down my face dried, and I moved on. Each time, I was ready to start the highly chaotic but deeply satisfying process again, again, and then again. This is what entrepreneurship is all about.

All these experiences in various industries made me an expert at helping people. So much so that I started to gain public notice. In 2015, I received an award from *Small Business Monthly* magazine for being a trailblazing executive Wonder Woman in the business industry. And more recently, in February 2025, I received another award for STL Top Business Advisor. It was all very exciting because I made it to the front cover both times! Each time was a testimony that I am making an impact.

However, remember that I am not that kind of risk-taker, and I did not want to start from scratch, so I spent some time crafting a solid plan and gathering resources for the creation of my own business. My comfort was finding tools, platforms, and systems that had already proven successful. I picked the ones I trusted the most and got the best results to bring into my consulting practice. I became a Certified EOS Implementer˚ and certified Kobe Consultant in 2018 and began working toward other certifications to integrate into my consulting practice. This made the process easier because I was not having to curate everything out of thin air. With these certifications in place, I felt confident that my practice would now have the impact to continue helping businesses.

In retrospect, it did not take long for the business to become a success. At around year two, I started to make a profit. However, during this space of success, I came upon a serious road bump: the global pandemic. The result? Everything that I had built up to, leading up to the pandemic,

I lost. I lost most of my clients and almost the business that I had worked on for the past two years. At this moment, I felt like I was on the edge of a cliff. Ready to jump. Ready to finally give up. It would have been so easy to do.

But I didn't jump. I talked to coaches and mentors who edged me back from the cliff. They reminded me that the whole world was going through this right now, and that I had the talent to persevere. I will forever be thankful for their support because it got me back on track. After this, I was able to sit down and think: *What's my marketing strategy now? What does it need to be in order for my business to make it through this period?* Through some changes to my marketing strategy, I ended up growing a business client base of remote businesses. These businesses were already accustomed to working remotely. They ended up being a great help because while my team was trying to learn Zoom, they had been using it for years! We had experts help train us. I also made the decision to invest in technology during a time when no one was spending money. This technology would make virtual appointments as comfortable as possible. Despite being on Zoom, I still wanted my clients to feel as if they were in my brick-and-mortar building. The high-end technology to make this happen ended up proving so successful that people were passing my name around and recommending me because I invested in the technology to give them the best remote experience possible.

I was able to not only survive during the pandemic but also thrive because I acquired enough remote business clients to get through the lockdown. I eventually returned to in-person consulting when the world went back to normal. I still believe my business is best served in person, but I'm proud that I was able to adapt to the virtual world. I still offer virtual services, which helps bring in more clients than I would have if I just remained in person.

Post pandemic, we are still going strong! We have the best clients, and I love assisting them not only with their professional lives but also with their personal ones. When I have a client come back and say that I helped make a difference in both aspects of their lives, that is the best reward for me. It is more than money can buy.

To anyone who is thinking of venturing down the path of entrepreneurship, I would advise you to avoid immediately saying no to the paths that your heart leads you down in the moment. Trust your intuition! Those paths have different opportunities that present themselves, and they will allow you to hone in and discover your real passion. You may not always get the opportunity that puts you in the right place at the right time. Sometimes you need to take those paths that lead you on detours. The place you are supposed to land will only be revealed by saying yes to these different paths and opportunities. I didn't start in the industry I am in today right away. It took several different opportunities to eventually arrive at my destination. And that's okay! I have loved my journey as much as my destination.

It is also essential to ensure that you are not alone on your entrepreneurial journey. Make sure you find your coach and tribe who will support you when you need it most. You will most likely face those moments when you feel like jumping off the edge of that cliff, so it is essential to have those people to pull you back. Find the person who will be that encourager to you. Find the person who will be that challenger to you. Find the person who will be that coach and mentor to you. Finding your tribe and following your heart are the best ways to launch your "accidental" incredible entrepreneurial journey. I'm proof of that!

With over 30 years of executive and entrepreneurial leadership experience, Shea helps entrepreneurial business leaders "Get Real" about their organizations in business and in life. Through her work, she equips leadership teams with the mindset and structure needed to elevate their business and ultimately thrive in their personal, family, and business lives.

Shea guides leadership teams in implementing the Entrepreneurial Operating System™ (EOS®), a proven system with practical tools designed to clarify priorities, instill discipline, and drive execution with focus and accountability.

Menagerie Coaching and PurpleCo.Biz, LLC also supports executive leaders with executive coaching, right-fit hiring, predictable revenue growth, and creating sustainable business growth.

Shea believes that real, lasting change doesn't happen by chance—it requires intention, strategy, and commitment. While the process may be challenging, the rewards are transformative.

Please scan the QR code to connect with this author.

## Crystal Allen Dallas

# Leading with Purpose

Representation matters. Seeing women—of all colors, ages, and sexualities—lead and thrive in their careers leaves a lasting imprint on children. As I reflect on my experience of becoming a force in business, I'm reminded of the powerful examples of women leaders I witnessed throughout my life. Their presence showed me what was possible and planted the seeds of my own ambition. Growing up in church, I was surrounded by passionate women leaders who often created miracles with very little. They turned small donations into massive gifts that breathed life into the communities that they served. It was here that I learned the true meaning of service to all humanity. To be of some help to others has always filled me with so much joy. It taught me that when we collaborate, we can accomplish anything. It planted the seeds for the work I do today: building community through engagement.

At my first corporate job, a senior executive saw my potential and made sure others did too. A native New Yorker, she was bold, fearless, and didn't take no for an answer. One of my most vivid memories of her is when she volunteered me, without hesitation, to present in front of over 1,000 employees and a group of top executives visiting from across the country. I was terrified, but she looked at me and said, "Crystal, you know this community better than anyone else. Why wouldn't it be you?" She was right. I rose to the occasion, and the CEO personally praised my work and asked me to lead a special initiative.

That experience taught me the power of advocacy, confidence, and preparation. We all need someone who sees us, champions us, and helps us navigate the road ahead. Most importantly, it taught me that mindset matters—when you believe you can, you will. And when you know it, show it. It's not bragging if you can back it up.

Another phenomenal woman leader who impacted my journey was a client who went out of her way to affirm my value. I wasn't sure what to expect when we first met, but I remember she was impressed that I arrived early and fully prepared. Her timeline was tight, and I was initially unsure whether my small firm could meet the demands. But we not only delivered, we exceeded expectations. That project turned into many more because she believed in my potential and challenged me to rise. To this day, she remains a trusted client, mentor, and example of what it means to lead with both excellence and intention.

Women have taught me to strive to be the best version of myself. However, their example was helped by an innate desire for greatness on my part. From an early age, I've carried a deep desire to leave every space better than I found it. The pursuit of excellence, innovation, and empowerment has always empowered me. Fueled by curiosity and a deep desire to understand how organizations function, I absorbed everything I could about marketing, finance, and strategic planning. People often talk about overnight success, but that's rarely the full story. What looks like a sudden breakthrough is usually the result of years of quiet perseverance, intentional growth, and behind-the-scenes work. The journey may not always be visible, but the foundation is built long before the spotlight ever arrives.

While many things have contributed to helping me achieve my goals, one of the most transformative was the bold decision to step away from a stable corporate career to pursue my vision—building a firm that centers equity, culture, and community in public engagement. That leap of faith marked a pivotal turning point, transforming me from an accomplished professional into a purpose-led entrepreneur.

Before founding my own company, I built a strong foundation in marketing, community engagement, and strategic partnerships through leadership roles at several prominent organizations. I served as Vice President of Resource Development at a regional nonprofit, where I led major fundraising initiatives and community investment strategies. At another regional organization, I focused on member engagement and regional economic development. I also worked with a hospitality company, where I managed public relations, community outreach, and brand communications for a portfolio of entertainment properties. These diverse experiences across the nonprofit, civic, and corporate sectors shaped my perspective on equity-centered engagement.

While I enjoyed my roles in the corporate world, I constantly found myself asking how businesses could operate more efficiently while also creating empowering spaces for everyone involved. That question became the spark that led me to start my own venture, Excel Business Concepts—a firm dedicated to bridging communities, culture, and communication to drive lasting impact.

Initially, the decision to found Excel Business Concepts arose from my desire to choose my own projects and people to work with, while having the flexibility to attend to my growing family. However, launching my own company was far from easy. I encountered the typical challenges that come with entrepreneurship: building a client base, figuring out how to position my services in a crowded market, and making ends meet in the early stages of a new venture. Additionally, as a Black female entrepreneur, I often faced biases, difficulties securing funding, and a feeling of underrepresentation in some of the professional circles I entered.

Through determination and strong reliance on my faith, I began forming partnerships with community organizations and delivering consistent results that spoke for themselves. Over time, Excel Business Concepts evolved from a small consulting firm into a firm known for its hands-on approach and dedication to helping clients translate their dreams into tangible business strategies. I always wanted Excel and its impact to be bigger than me. I realized that achieving my own business goals was only part of the equation. I have always been intentional about leveraging my position to uplift and guide others, especially women who faced similar social and economic barriers.

This commitment to helping other women has become integral to my leadership philosophy. Whether I am volunteering as a guest lecturer at local colleges, establishing community-based engagement programs, or speaking at conferences, I strive to share the knowledge, experiences, and practical advice that I wish I had earlier. I firmly believe that nobody reaches success on their own; we are all supported by networks, communities, and circles of trust that help us navigate obstacles.

My primary goal has been to impact the world with positive change. My company has given me an amazing platform to share my expertise, talent, passion, and live out my purpose. My responsibilities at Excel Business Concepts have grown. In the beginning, I was simply focused on generating enough business to support the life I was building for myself and my family. Today, I'm responsible not only for sustaining the company's operations but also for supporting a growing team—people who entrust me with their livelihoods and professional growth. I take that responsibility to heart.

Excel has become a kind of incubator, an environment where talent is nurtured and launched. Many of my team members have gone on to work for global agencies, and they often credit their time at Excel as instrumental in preparing them for the next level. I remember one team member in particular, a first-generation college graduate who dreamed of working at a specific agency but had been rejected multiple times. After spending a year at Excel, they landed that job with high praise. To this day, they tell me it was here they learned the unspoken rules of business—how to lead with excellence, build meaningful relationships, and view failure as a stepping stone, not a setback.

What I've come to realize is that Excel may not be everyone's forever home, and that's okay. My goal is to create a space where people feel seen, heard, and valued, and where they gain the confidence and experience to pursue their biggest ambitions. If I can offer that kind of exposure and growth, then I know I'm fulfilling my purpose as a leader.

Over the years, I have developed a mindset of continuous improvement, recognizing that personal and professional growth do not have a finish line. Leadership is not just about technical competence, either; it is also about emotional fortitude, resilience, and the ability to navigate complex interpersonal dynamics. I aim to be a role model for other aspiring female leaders, especially those from underrepresented communities. I want them to look at me and see the possibility of occupying leadership roles on a global scale. My ambition is not just personal advancement; it is communal. When one woman breaks a barrier or blazes a trail, she paves the way for countless others. I plan to carry that responsibility forward.

In developing my leadership style, I have come to understand how critical self-awareness and ethical grounding are for guiding an organization or community successfully. Everything I have accomplished at Excel Business Concepts so far, I have done through a combination of business acumen, emotional intelligence, and a relentless focus on client success.

One of the most defining accomplishments was securing a major infrastructure contract for my firm. This opportunity gave us access to high-impact work and allowed us to scale our engagement strategies to deliver meaningful, regional outcomes. Serving as the top leader of a regional nonprofit organization was another defining chapter. It expanded my capacity as a community leader and provided a powerful platform to champion women's leadership, service, and systemic change. These experiences, taken together, deepened my commitment to purpose-driven work and affirmed the power of leading with both strategy and heart.

At the core of it all is my identity—as a Black woman, mother, and advocate. My lived experiences continue to fuel my unwavering commitment to equity, authenticity, and elevating underrepresented voices. That clarity of purpose has not only shaped the mission of Excel Business Concepts, but it has also redefined what success looks like for me: creating impact that is both measurable and meaningful.

To all the women reading this who aspire to be leaders in their field, it is important to remember that there is no traffic jam on the extra mile, so don't be afraid to go further, do more, and lead with intention. Choose joy. Pursue what aligns with your purpose. And always remember *you are enough, just as you are.*

Here are three of my favorite leadership gems—guiding principles I live by and often share with others:

### 1. The Power of Cultivating Relationships

Understand the power of cultivating authentic relationships. One of the most valuable lessons I've learned is that success is often rooted in the connections you build and nurture. Don't approach relationships as mere transactions; see them as opportunities for mutual growth and genuine support. Take time to truly learn about others, understand their journey, and seek ways to add value. When you lead with intention and generosity, meaningful and lasting relationships will follow.

### 2. Leverage the Growth Dynamic

Embrace the growth dynamic. What got you here won't be enough to keep you here. Stay curious. Be intentional about going the extra mile to learn, stretch, and evolve. The most valuable opportunities often lie in the details, not the spotlight. While speed can be useful, don't underestimate the power of a steady, deliberate pace. Growth isn't always flashy. It's often quiet, disciplined, and consistent. What matters most is reaching your goal with integrity and purpose.

### 3. Celebrate!

Celebrate the moments. As women leaders, we often move so quickly toward the next goal that we forget to honor the progress we've already made. I've learned that it's just as important to pause, reflect, and acknowledge the wins—big or small. You set a goal and achieved it; that's worth celebrating. You are worthy of recognition, joy, and pride in your journey. Don't rush past your milestones. Let them remind you of your power and purpose.

My path has been shaped by intention, resilience, and an unwavering belief in the power of purpose-driven work. From my early influences to my corporate experiences and entrepreneurial leap, each chapter has deepened my commitment to equity, leadership, and community. Founding Excel Business Concepts wasn't just a professional decision—it was a personal calling to create space for impact, inclusion, and innovation. Along the way, I've learned that real success is not about arriving quickly, but about growing deliberately and lifting others as you rise. My hope is that my story inspires others to lead boldly, pursue their purpose, and never underestimate the power of one voice to drive meaningful change.

Crystal Allen Dallas is the founder and Chief Engagement Officer of Excel Business Concepts, a strategic communications firm based in St. Louis specializing in public engagement, branding, and equity-centered outreach. With a passion for building stronger communities through inclusive communication, Crystal leads initiatives that amplify voices, foster collaboration, and drive measurable impact. Under her leadership, Excel has contributed to high-profile infrastructure projects.

Crystal is also a civic leader and advocate for women in leadership and has held leadership roles across numerous regional boards. She is the recipient of honors such as the *St. Louis Business Journal's* 40 Under 40 and a graduate of the Small Business Administration's (SBA) T.H.R.I.V.E. program. Through her work, Crystal champions purposeful engagement, believing that community-driven solutions lead to more equitable and sustainable outcomes.

When Crystal is not working, you can find her enjoying shopping for unique pieces to add to her wardrobe and art collection, traveling, and spending time with her family.

Please scan the QR code to connect with this author.

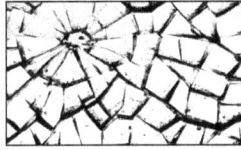

**Susanne Evens**

# To Catch the American Dream

I didn't come to America chasing a dream. I came because love, duty, and sacrifice gave me no other choice.

What I didn't realize then was that life would ask me to lose everything—my native country, community, marriage, and sense of safety—so I could find the fiercest parts of myself: my voice, purpose, and the quiet fire that refuses to quit.

That fire became my compass. And over time, it led me not just to build a business, but to build a life that matters.

## Where I Come From

Growing up in Germany meant structure, discipline, and a deep respect for tradition, where rules were clear.

It also gave me parents who had survived the unimaginable horrors of World War II and still managed to raise me with love, an open mind, and a curiosity about the world. Summers were spent exploring other countries and cultures, planting in me the early seeds of what would become a lifelong passion for language.

At sixteen, I placed a small ad in the local newspaper offering translation services. One businessman responded. He came to our home, sat at the dining room table with me and my parents, and asked me to translate a business letter. I did. Before he left, he placed money on the table.

He had no idea what he had done. But I did. That moment lit a spark in me that I would never forget. I immersed myself in the study of languages: English, French, Italian, Russian, and Spanish, and I obtained a degree as a Foreign Language Correspondent. A Foreign Language Correspondent is a professional who handles international communication, translation, and interpretation for a company or organization, using their fluency in one or more foreign languages.

This degree landed me my first career with Hewlett-Packard Germany, translating internal communication. After a few years, I resigned as I was getting ready to relocate to the United States.

## Becoming a Military Wife

When I married a U.S. soldier, I thought I understood what commitment meant. But nothing prepares you for the constant upheaval of military life.

We moved every 15 to 18 months: Nashville, Tennessee; Ft. Polk, Louisiana; Monterey, California; Ft. Huachuca, Arizona; Ft. Hood, Texas; and back to Germany again. During the Iran-Iraq War, we lived off-base in Germany and were ordered to check under our cars for bombs every morning. That's not a metaphor. That was my reality.

And through it all—through the deployments, the worry, the isolation—I put my own ambitions on hold. There was simply no space to dream when survival was the priority.

But deep down, the spark still burned.

Some interesting moments during my husband's military career included working for a real estate attorney in Carmel, California. Clint Eastwood's real estate attorney! Eastwood was the mayor of Carmel at the time and was one of several celebrities in my world. I also stood in line at the post office with Doris Day and enjoyed a private tour of Bob Dylan's home on the Pacific Ocean. While living in Ft. Hood, Texas, I also worked for an attorney in downtown Killeen, Texas, where "adult service providers" strolled up and down the street. While stationed in Germany, I organized a collection of food and clothing for Russian orphans among the military personnel.

## Life Unraveling

When my husband retired, we settled in his hometown of St. Louis with our two young daughters. I hoped we would finally find stability. Instead, I found heartbreak.

Our marriage ended in a bitter divorce. I was alone in a foreign country, far from my family, unable to return to Germany because of custody laws. I had no job, no network, and no safety net.

Some days, I sat on the floor and cried after putting the girls to bed. But I made a promise to myself in those dark moments: I would not give up. I would build something from the ashes.

I didn't have a grand vision. I had grit. I had passion. And I had persistence.

## Rebuilding From the Ground Up

I started small. I worked for an attorney during the week and transcribed medical reports on the weekends. Then came a break. An international firm needed someone who spoke German. I got the job.

But more importantly, I restarted my old side business: German Language Communications.

There were no guarantees. No roadmaps. Just me, a computer, a phone line, a fax machine, and a deep knowing that I was meant for more. That dream began to take shape and take root.

Then, life surprised me again.

I remarried. I found my soulmate. And at nearly 40, I became pregnant again. We moved up our wedding so I could walk down the aisle before I walked into the delivery room.

On our wedding night, Bruce Springsteen and his wife stepped into our hotel elevator—yes, really. Some of our wedding guests had even left early for his concert. I remember saying to Bruce, "Now we can tell them we spent our wedding night with The Boss." He laughed. We all did.

Before our son was born, I decided to resign from my full-time job during my parental leave so I could stay home with my newborn. Six weeks of maternity leave were not enough for me and my newborn, and just the thought of an unsupportive boss made me cringe.

Unlike the United States, Germany provides comprehensive maternity and parental leave policies. Maternity leave lasts 14 weeks, with flexible timing for medical or job-related reasons. Parental leave lets either parent take up to three years off.

Two weeks into my parental leave, I received a certified letter stating that the firm was closing. To my surprise, it included generous severance pay.

This was my big AHA moment! After all my hardships—being a military wife, enduring a painful divorce, and being unable to move back home—the American Dream of owning my own full-time business was finally becoming real. I decided to turn my part-time business into a full-time venture. I wanted the flexibility to manage my own schedule while being present for my children as a stay-at-home mom. It was important to me to balance my professional goals with family life, and running my own business allowed me to do both on my own terms. It was challenging with a baby, teenagers, and no business connections, but I had learned persistence from my parents. My mom was a business owner, and as a young girl, I watched her work tirelessly and persevere through every challenge without ever giving up.

In 2000, German Language Communications was rebranded to AAA Translation, Inc., as a long-term client requested additional languages beyond German. As an entrepreneur, you just lean into it. AAA

Translation turned into a full-service foreign language translation and global consulting firm, working on every continent except Antarctica. We have not cracked the Penguin language yet.

We were virtual before it was cool. We kept our model lean, smart, and value-driven. Every day, my team and I enjoy working across cultures, countries, and causes. It's never boring. It's never easy. But it is always meaningful.

Twenty-five years later, we are still virtual, and we strategically outsource non-core functions to focus our resources and expertise on what we do best—translation and interpreting. Each day presents a rich opportunity to expand our knowledge and understanding through the diverse experiences, perspectives, and traditions of the many countries, cultures, and individuals we collaborate with. Whether through language, customs, or unique approaches to problem-solving, we are continually inspired and challenged to grow, both personally and professionally. This constant exchange not only deepens our global awareness but also strengthens our ability to connect, adapt, and thrive in an increasingly interconnected world.

## From Homesick to Homegrown

Still, part of me missed Germany. That changed when I stumbled across the **St. Louis–Stuttgart Sister Cities (SLSSC)** booth at a local festival. I learned that SLSSC promotes business, cultural, and student exchanges between our cities. It aims to foster peace through mutual respect and cooperation, one individual and one community at a time.

Stuttgart was just 70 kilometers from my hometown in Germany. Feeling inspired, I started volunteering. Eventually, I became president in 1996, and I have just announced my retirement after 20 years.

Through Sister Cities, I played a key role in successfully introducing and establishing two German companies to St. Louis. I hosted mayors and dignitaries. I built bridges between my past and my present. I gained valuable experience in fundraising and developed effective strategies to support our initiatives. Finally, I stopped feeling torn between two homes and started realizing I could belong to both.

Giving back—through business, mentorship, and cultural connection—has become my purpose.

## A Proud Moment in 2008—Becoming a United States Citizen

Becoming a U.S. citizen is a deeply proud and emotional milestone, a moment that marks the culmination of hard work, perseverance, and a profound commitment to a new homeland. It symbolizes not just the fulfillment of a long journey, but also the beginning of new opportunities, rights, and responsibilities. Standing alongside 69 others from around the world, taking the Oath of Allegiance, and officially becoming part of the American story is an unforgettable experience, one that embodies hope, freedom, and the promise of a better future.

## What I've Learned

People often ask me how I made it. The truth is, I didn't have a plan. I had:

- **Passion** that refused to burn out,
- **People** who showed up at the right time,
- And **Persistence** that carried me through every moment.

If I could whisper something to my younger self, it would be this: *You don't have to know where the road ends. Just take the next brave step. Don't be afraid to ask for help—it's a sign of strength, not a weakness.*

Trust yourself when no one else does. Keep learning. Keep adapting. And always—always—build relationships rooted in trust, not just transactions, and mentor others to help them grow and prosper in their own journeys. That's how you build something that lasts. That's how you turn struggle into strength.

That's how you chase—and catch—the American Dream.

Susanne Evens was born and raised in Germany. She has a degree as a Foreign Language Correspondent.

Susanne is the president of St. Louis—Stuttgart Sister Cities, serves on the board of Titan 100, World Trade Center St. Louis, St. Louis Forum, the German Heritage Society, and is a mentor for the St. Louis Mosaic Project International Mentoring Program.

Some of Susanne's awards include the 2022 and 2023 St. Louis Titan 100, 2022 Top Women Business Owner—*St. Louis Small Business Monthly*; 2021 Enterprising Women of the Year—*Enterprising Women Magazine*; 2017 St. Louis Mosaic Immigrant Entrepreneur Award—St. Louis Mosaic Project; 2016 "Top 100 St. Louisans to Know to Succeed in Business" *St. Louis Small Business Monthly*; and the 2013 Friedrich Hecker Freedom Award—German American Heritage Society of Saint Louis.

When Susanne is not working, she enjoys traveling, power walking, hiking, gardening, mentoring, and horseback riding whenever possible.

Please scan the QR code to connect with this author.

**Lorri Rippelmeyer**

# Count Yourself In

January 2015 marked a new point in my professional life. After nearly three decades of trying to dismantle and shatter the ever-resilient glass ceiling, the structure finally gave way, at least for me. It was a tough fight, one that took more energy and years in my life than I care to think about.

Standing in front of my colleagues at a firm meeting and announcing my exciting news, with victory tears welling up in my eyes, I knew that every minute I had spent reaching my goal was *so* worth it. The glass-shattering news I shared with everyone was that I had been made a partner. As I received a series of congratulations and beautiful support from my colleagues, I was happy, but there was a part of me that couldn't believe that I had finally made it. Looking back, it took some time for reality to set in!

I started working at a CPA firm in 1988, a time when the term "female partner" might have been considered an oxymoron. During the 1980s, more women than at any point in history entered the workforce, so my quest started in a time of better opportunities for women than in previous generations. Media, television, and movies all began featuring women in roles unheard of before, a move that also made women more visible in their work and communities, too. The 1980s were the start of a period of change and growing opportunities for women, changes that made it possible for women to begin to reach levels of greater equality. There was so much work to do at the time, and almost 50 years later, there is still work to do.

While corporate America became the first to promote women in the workforce, professional services firms, including CPA firms like mine, were slower to adapt. Once a boy's club, accounting today is a career of choice for many women. In fact, today, more women than men study accounting in college and enter the profession. However, while change has occurred, leadership at many firms remains obstinately male-dominated. While the gap is less than when I first started my tenure at the CPA firm, we have yet to close it. During my early years, being the only woman in a boardroom was not a rarity, but the norm. The firm opened its doors in the 1960s, but it took until 2014 to elect its first female partner. Today, female partners make up approximately 25% with many others in line for partner and yet others in non-partner leadership roles.

It would be taking the easy route to blame the lack of female representation in professional services firms and other industries on societal sexism only. Yes, sexism played a role here, but there was more to it. Throughout years of working at the firm, talking to my female colleagues and to women climbing the ranks in other careers, I discovered an incredible thing: Women were counting themselves out for the opportunity. While less prevalent than in my time, in ways, I believe some still do.

Why did women self-select out of positions of leadership? Why did they feel the job requirements were so beyond their reach that they didn't even *try* for the brass ring? What could I do to help these women count themselves in? These questions caused me to set out on a quest to answer them, a quest that would prove to be transformative for my career and my understanding of what it takes to bring about much-needed change to the status quo.

The quest began as soon as I joined the firm as an associate in January 1988. I hadn't worked for a CPA firm prior to this, so this job was my first foray into the world of public accounting. I started in accounting services, which involved accounting/bookkeeping work for clients. The group was 99% women. Several people in this group were college graduates. They started in accounting services and then moved on to tax. At that time, the position was a stepping stone for larger roles.

While the tax and audit groups had more men, there were also women, but no partners, and few held high positions. Despite this reality, I aspired to move to the tax department. To accomplish this goal, I went to night school at Webster University to earn a bachelor's degree. Working full-time and going to night school was a challenge to say the least! This part of my life felt like it took several decades. In reality, it took about nine years until I graduated in May 2004.

Did I take a much-deserved and needed break after getting my bachelor's? Not so much! After this achievement, the next goal was to start studying and working toward taking the CPA exam.

While studying for the exam, I hit yet *another* detour. The required college hours to sit for the CPA exam changed from 120 hours (usually, the number for a bachelor's degree) to 150 hours (the number required for a master's degree). Since I had to get the extra hours to sit for the exam, my new goal was to get a master's degree. I started sitting for the computerized CPA exam in the summer of 2006 and passed the fourth and final part in the summer of 2007. At last, I was an official CPA!

My goal for nearly 20 years had been achieved. *How much more time will I have on my hands since I was no longer a studen*t, I thought incredulously. However, I soon discovered that my goal of becoming a CPA was really just the beginning of a bigger dream in the works. One that would affect not just me, but all my women colleagues.

The next step to elevating my career was becoming a partner. This is a perfectly logical step to take after you get certified in the accounting industry. Logical, yes, but feasible for a woman? That would be harder. As I looked around my firm for female role models in executive and partner positions, I found none. There was no older and wiser woman who had struggled with the same obstacles I did, but made it through anyway. No one who could advise me on what ingredients were needed to make the secret sauce that would grant me my seat at the table.

While I didn't have anyone to tell me how to get that seat at the table, I was not alone. I had my female colleagues by my side; women who were all in the same boat as me. In particular, I had my female colleague Donna, who headed our marketing department. While not a CPA, she understood the misogyny in the accounting industry, in all industries, really, on all levels. We turned our angst into action in 2009.

Timing is everything, and ours was perfect. At the same time, we were starting a women's group at the firm, the American Institute of Certified Public Accountants (AICPA) was also taking a hard look at increasing leadership roles for women in all firms across the country. We got the opportunity to be part of a series of AICPA workshops designed for that purpose. While we were the smallest firm in the group, we were also the most engaged. We had the most to prove; the most to gain.

On a local level, we met with women who had reached partner status at their respective law firms. It was through our conversations that I had my suspicion confirmed that sexism was not the only culprit in holding women back. There were also internal factors to blame. Most women in accounting and law, it appeared, were not seeking executive and partner positions because they did not believe they could fulfill all the duties needed to succeed in those positions. They were the ones saying no, the ones not asking, not seeking the opportunities, not pushing. They were counting themselves out.

To become a partner, you need to be responsible for bringing in business to the firm, maintaining relationships with existing clients, and building relationships with referral sources and business leaders in the community. These duties entail spending a large amount of time in the office, networking, and attending industry events. Many of these take place beyond business hours. These were some of the factors keeping women from striving to become partners: they didn't and still don't believe they have the time to accomplish them. When a woman with family responsibilities comes home from her full-time job, she is met with a second shift: taking care of her family and all the responsibilities that come with that. Several of my counterparts took on the task of doing it all: career, family, leadership, mentorship, community, and profession to help us in our quest. It wasn't easy then, and still isn't.

Refusing to give up the fight, Donna and I decided to broaden our campaign and concentrate on business development to bring more women business owners and women in business to the firm as clients and referral sources. This brought unprecedented success! We also succeeded in getting more women onto nonprofit and professional boards. At the same time, we sought to get women to be part of women's groups in the community, such as the Professional Women's Alliance (PWA). Little by little, we turned these goals into reality.

Our efforts were proving successful, and we started to gain recognition. My colleague and I went on to gain many awards, including the Most Influential Business Women. Additionally, we assisted in starting the Women's Initiative at LEA Global, an international organization of accounting firms to which our company belongs. Donna and I worked the women's group within the LEA organization each year to meet at annual conferences and discuss what different firms were doing as it related to women's groups in their firms. Some years, we even arranged for speakers at the annual conference to talk to the women's group, and we were speakers for other organizations and firms.

It's a great feeling knowing that I was partially responsible for bringing a substantial number of women (professionals and clients) into the firm. I also proved myself worthy by bringing in a new category of clients—athletes and entertainers. Sports are an important part of my life, as I come from an athletic family. My father was a baseball player, and my brother, Brad, was also a baseball player and is now an investment advisor who has a focus on working with athletes. Brad sent several clients my way. I knew how to navigate the complex and unique world of taxes for athletes, and I helped train other CPAs to work with them.

Working with athletes or people in the entertainment industry requires a special set of communication skills. Sometimes you deal with the athlete or entertainment person directly, but other times you communicate with their agents or spouses. Much of the time, I needed to use my soft skills and be a sympathetic listener, hand holder, and counselor. Soft skills, incidentally, that women are better at and have more experience with providing. Our clients in this industry ended up showing that female CPAs can have an advantage over males because they tend to have more experience with successfully balancing soft and hard skills, something very much needed with this clientele. Once again, my work was proving that women belonged and deserved a place in accounting. In hindsight, it is funny to think that I was the one responsible for bringing in so many clients in the sports, arts, and entertainment industries, industries that are very male-dominated! If we are keeping score, I am two for two!

As stated earlier, I was finally recognized for all my accomplishments when I was made a partner in 2015. I may have won the fight for myself, but as a partner, I have kept up the fight for others by actively recruiting more women to the firm and encouraging them to aspire to high positions of power. Personal success has not become my stopping point;

women have helped me shatter that glass ceiling, and I will continue to help others. I have learned a bit of the secret sauce that gets women their place at the table, and I want to share it to ensure that more women aspire to and achieve a place in the boardroom. If you are wondering about the women who joined me on the original journey, the good news is that most became partners and/or members of the C-suite. It fills me with pride knowing that I made a significant crack in the glass ceiling at my company. I officially retired last year, but I continue to assist with clients on an as-needed basis, and I continue to support women at all levels through my work on non-profit boards and mentoring.

My advice for other women is to stop counting themselves out and instead count themselves in. Know that you can confidently rise to the top of this or any other profession or industry if you join with other women to defeat the odds. It may seem overwhelming at first. It will take time. But, most importantly, it will be worth it. Continue making those cracks, not just for yourself, but for all women, until there is no ceiling.

For more than 30 years, Lorri has played an integral role in the accounting industry. She joined a CPA firm located in St. Louis in 1988 and progressed to becoming a partner in tax and a leader of the firm's Sports, Arts, & Entertainment Group. Lorri also helped form the firm's Women's Initiative, a group devoted to encouraging professional women to aim for higher leadership positions in their industries.

Lorri worked toward her bachelor's and master's degrees and prepared for the CPA exam, all while working full-time! She holds a B.S. in Accounting from Webster University and an M.S. in Accountancy from Southern Illinois University-Edwardsville.

In 2012, the *St. Louis Business Journal* named Lorri one of St. Louis's Most Influential Business Women. Before she retired in December 2024, she was awarded the STL Top Business Advisor by *Small Business Monthly*.

Lorri's hobbies include spending time with family and friends, traveling, enjoying life, and volunteering.

Please scan the QR code to connect with this author.

**Esmeralda Aharon**

# Combat Boots to Business

From a young age, I learned what it meant to build something beautiful with my own hands. I was just thirteen years old when I began taking floral arranging classes. My mother also wanted to learn something new, but she decided on cake decorating. Those Saturday mornings became a space where creativity bloomed, and confidence took root. For two years, I studied the art of floral design. Why? My mother wanted me to learn a trade that I would always have in my back pocket, just in case. By the time my *quinceañera* came, I had designed and created all the decorations with a precision that takes seasoned stylists years to accomplish.

That experience changed everything. It was not just about flowers. It was the first time I saw myself as a creator, a visionary, and a problem-solver. After that celebration, I began designing floral arrangements for family and friends, slowly stepping into entrepreneurship without even knowing the word for it. Later, I worked at a floral shop and realized how much my little hands were making for the florist while I was paid minimum wage. While this hobby gave me joy in taking someone's vision and turning it into something tangible and meaningful, I realized that my skills were more valuable than what I was receiving. Knowing the value of my work, I quit working at the floral shop, but that early taste of ownership and creativity became the seed for the leader I would later become.

Years later, that same spirit carried me through 26 years in the U.S. Air Force. I served as an Airman, Non-Commissioned Officer, and Senior Non-Commissioned Officer in the Chaplain Corps. Through each rank, I grew in responsibility by managing millions of dollars in resources to include multiple facilities and supporting Catholic, Jewish, and Protestant worship communities and councils, among other religions and practices. Leading diverse religious affairs teams and serving military families across the globe were the activities *du jour*. Serving in this career field instilled in me a wide range of skills that have proven invaluable in entrepreneurship. I learned the art of compassionate leadership, how to meet people where they are, to listen deeply, and to hold space for their stories without judgment. Mediating conflict, fostering belonging, and building systems of spiritual and emotional care were activities in which I occupied myself. Besides planning, organizing, and delivering programs and events, I facilitated ceremonies, memorials, and retreats: each one requiring precision, empathy, and the ability to lead under emotional strain and at times, in contingency environments.

Entrepreneurs require great communication skills, and through my role in Religious Affairs, I became a skilled communicator, designing marketing materials for chapel and installation events; skills I now apply to promoting our business. This leadership position kept me on my toes and taught me patience regardless of the customer base and persistence in all areas of responsibility, where I needed to discuss and justify every cent received and expensed. Among the many areas in which I excelled, financial oversight emerged as one of my greatest strengths, as I managed appropriated, non-appropriated, and morale and welfare funds with integrity. I directed these systems with care and created the template for other installations to ensure ethical standards in efficiency, integrity, and logistics across diverse teams and stakeholders. Every element of my work demanded attention to detail, cross-cultural sensitivity, discretion, and ethical decision-making skills that now support every aspect of running a values-based business.

And yes, my floral arranging skills came full circle. Those early lessons I took as a girl became part of my service. I used them to lovingly decorate chapel altars for funerals, honoring both the young and the old with beauty and care. I discovered how to carry grief while still compassionately leading through theirs. In moments of great joy, I climbed ladders to place the perfectly shaped tree topper bow on the Christmas tree, and during fall festivals, I transformed parade fields with pumpkins and seasonal foliage. However, most people saw the final touch, not the story behind it. But I knew. I was the same young girl who once created her own *quinceañera* decorations, now serving others through my first creative love, bringing beauty and comfort when it mattered most.

Military life taught me more than wearing a uniform and representing my country; it taught me discipline, resilience, compassion, and operational excellence. Leading during crises in and out of the continental United States empowered me to serve with dignity, respect, and professionalism, while stewarding complex systems with integrity. When I retired, I knew that leadership was not something to be left behind. It was something I was bringing into the next chapter of my life—Esmeralda 2.0.

This next chapter began with promoting an incredible skincare, healthcare, and home care line by Atomy. People listened to me. They trusted me. They joined me. Then I attended a gala where I met Lusnail Rondón Haberberger, who is both the founder and CEO of LUZCO Technologies. She asked me, "What is your business?" I explained I work in higher education, and I am a doctoral student, yet she asked me again, "But what is *your* business?" She reminded me that I was a Latina and Latinas are entrepreneurs. This conversation lingered in my mind, and I found myself repeatedly reflecting on Lusnail's question.

For years, I had worked for Uncle Sam. Perhaps it was finally time that I worked for myself. It was this conversation and many others with my friend Gabriela Ramirez-Arellano that gave birth to Latinas Rising LLC. As co-founders, we have created a space where Latinas and allies can be seen, supported, and celebrated. Our first order of business was to launch our anthology, *Calladitas Rising: Reclaiming Your Power, Strength, and Voice.* This anthology was personal. It included 32 Latinas who said, *calladita no mas,* silent no more, which stems from the phrase *calladita te vez mas bonita,* you look prettier when you are quiet. In Latin American culture, women have been *calladitas* for generations. This phrase was told to most women regardless of their country of origin and social status. It was said to my great-grandmother, her mother, my grandmother, my mother, my aunts, cousins, etc. Since I work in higher education, I knew that I needed to research this phenomenon and discovered very little research on the topic and the impact of this phrase on our community.

Through conversations with female medical students, I realized that, regardless of the year we are living in, this cultural phenomenon still lives and remains ingrained in our DNA. It is through writing about it that employers, colleagues, classmates, etc., can truly understand the Latina psyche. It is important to understand that even while Latinas are earning higher education degrees and "sitting at the table," they may still be hearing this phrase in their head. This is not theory, but very much reality for many Latinas.

This revelation encouraged my friend and me to launch this project, and boy, we were worried that we would be unable to find enough women who were willing to tell their stories. Yet, we were successful. We were persistent and knew this topic needed to be out in the open. In September 2024, we published *Calladitas Rising,* hitting Best Selling Status prior to launch and #1 Best-Selling Status within three hours of launch. It reached International Best-Selling Status within nine hours of launch, and #1

International Best-Selling Status within 16 hours of launch! All in all, it reached Best #1 Selling Status in the United States, Canada, and Brazil for a total of 59 best-selling categories, including 25 ranking #1!

To date, this anthology continues to make waves. We sparked a movement of Latinas that declared, "It stops with me!" It has opened doors for critical conversations in higher education and beyond, challenging systems that have long overlooked our stories. We knew our work was far from over. Latinas Rising now offers two inclusive memberships open to all women. Through our Innovator Collective and Influencer Circle, we are building bridges for those still finding their way. We are reclaiming space, creating platforms for voices long silenced, and offering authorship opportunities that empower women to speak their truths, own their narratives, and step boldly into leadership.

The women who join us are rising and lifting others as they climb on their own terms, in their own voice, and with full ownership of their power. And in the process, we are arranging a beautiful bouquet of voices, each distinct, flourishing, and radiant, that come together in collective strength. This work is more urgent now than ever before. We are currently living in a time when women's voices are being suppressed by deeply rooted systems of oppression, both in the military, an institution I have proudly served, and in the business world, which I now call home. It will take all of us to rise together, to say we and our voices matter. Gone are the days of staying silent and just looking pretty. We will raise our voices and never turn back.

Entrepreneurship, for me, is not a detour from service; it is a continuation of it. It is how I live out my values. It is how I am lifting others as I climb, which includes creating an inaugural Latinas Rising Scholarship. Our growing company presented its first scholarship to a young Latina to assist her in her academic journey toward becoming a physician. Not only did she receive the financial award, but she also joined our Innovator

Collective to receive mentorship and support as she rises. It gives me great joy to know that in less than two years, we are making a difference in the personal and professional lives of the women we are serving and lifting. Together, we are truly rising!

The girl who arranged her own *quinceañera* flowers became a woman who now arranges spaces for healing, growth, and transformation. Esmeralda 2.0 uses her voice to uplift others and graciously embraces the honor of being an unsung heroine of business, not for the titles I hold, but for the legacy I am cultivating in *comunidad* with so many others. Other incredible unsung heroines include Debi Robedeau-Corrie, the compiler of this anthology, and my dear friend and collaborator, Gabriela. Together, we are weaving a legacy of resilience, where every story shared becomes a thread of empowerment for the next generation.

If you are searching for a space that sees you, values you, and welcomes your voice, join us. Our Latinas Rising *familia* is open for business. Like when I served on active duty, I continue to lead with heart, discipline, and purpose, committed to building something greater than myself, and intentionally lifting others, like you, to rise. Your entrepreneurial dreams are not too big. Your voice is not too loud. Join us, and one day you will see that the very things that set you apart will become the reasons others find their strength. The road to bringing your business to life may be steep, marked by silence, grief, sacrifice, and systems designed to diminish your light, but keep rising. Not despite those struggles, but because of them. Join us because sisterhood is powerful. Healing is collective. Leadership does not require others' permission. Speak even when your voice trembles and write even when doubt lingers. Create and hold space for others, for your purpose was never meant to serve you alone. Together, let us rise. Together, let us help others bloom.

Esmeralda Aharon, M.A., is a retired U.S. Air Force combat veteran, keynote speaker, international best-selling author, and doctoral student in higher education. As Religious Affairs Senior Noncommissioned Officer (SNCO), she provided strategic-level support for the religious and spiritual needs of service members, their families, and the command structure. Her career bridges military leadership, higher education, and entrepreneurship.

She co-founded Latinas Rising LLC, a consulting firm focused on elevating women's voices through mentorship, authorship, and leadership development. As program director at Saint Louis University School of Medicine, Esmeralda advances health equity, belonging, and social justice. A recipient of the Spirit of the Four Chaplains, the Hispanic Lifetime Achievement Award, and the President's Volunteer Service Award, she has been invited twice to share her expertise as a mentor for Mentoring Monday with the *St. Louis Business Journal*.

In her downtime, Esmeralda enjoys yoga and photography. You can find several of her photographs featured at the Grafton Art Gallery.

Please scan the QR code to connect with this author.

## Gabriela Ramírez-Arellano

# Where My Voice Lives Now

For years, I stayed this way—keeping my head down, trying not to draw attention.

I wish I had the language of a poet to explain what it's like to be an immigrant—to put into words the way you can love two countries with all your heart and still feel like neither fully claims you. To capture the constant negotiation between pride and pain, between wanting to blend in and longing to be seen. That's the part of my story I carry into every room I walk into as a leader, mentor, and entrepreneur. It's the years of fitting in, then standing out, then reclaiming my voice—the voice I now refuse to silence.

At the beginning of my professional journey, I felt like a woman trying to survive. In 2012, at 43 years old, I was starting over, navigating a painful divorce while raising three teenagers and looking for my first real job. I had an MBA, and still couldn't find work. My confidence was low, my identity shaken. I didn't know what came next—only that I had to keep going.

How did I get here? Well, to fully answer that question, it is necessary to go back to the beginning…

I was five years old when my parents brought my sister Veronica and me to Disneyland. It was a magical vacation, and although I don't remember a lot of it, I am sure we saw Mickey Mouse, rode the teacups, sang "It's a Small World," and took pictures with Cinderella. Everything around me, the smells and lights, felt bright, safe, and full of joy. We had no idea that this trip would become more than a vacation.

I don't know how it happened, just that my dad was offered a job, and we stayed. My parents made the decision quietly, with the kind of seriousness I now understand only as an adult—the weight of choosing a better life for your children, even when it means leaving behind everything you know.

In those early years in California, my memories are hazy. I can't recall the exact streets or all the faces, but I do remember this—we fit in. Everywhere we turned, people looked like us, spoke Spanish like us, and ate the same foods we did. The mercados smelled like home. The music at family gatherings was the same music we heard at weddings and fiestas in Mexico. My mother cooked our favorite dishes, and we never felt like we had to explain who we were.

It wasn't until 1984, when we moved to Troy, Missouri, that I realized we were different. California had been a place where my language was a bridge; in Troy, it became a barrier. People would ask me, "What are you?" or "What are you mixed with?" as if my existence needed to be explained. Sometimes, when they overheard me speaking Spanish, they told me to "speak English." In those moments, I felt my cheeks burn and my stomach tighten. It wasn't just about language—it was about being told that a part of me was unacceptable, and therefore, that *I* was unacceptable.

I always found a way to explain the dirty looks and hurtful words to my mother, and I'd make something up. Protecting her from those small cruelties felt more important than speaking my own hurt. I learned to make myself invisible—not because I didn't love who I was, but because invisibility felt safer.

Fast forward several years, and this kind of invisibility followed me into my career…

There was fear. A lot of it. But I couldn't afford to wait until I felt ready. I needed to act, to rebuild. That's when I signed up for a business class through ProsperUS in southwest Detroit. I didn't go to that class with a business plan in hand. I went because I needed a way forward. I didn't know what kind of business I would start—only that I was meant to be entrepreneurial, and I hoped the class would help me shape an idea that could put food on the table.

Before I really thought about what was happening, I was invited to develop the curriculum in both English and Spanish, then to teach it, and eventually to coach the participants. And somewhere in that journey, I realized that entrepreneurship wasn't just a business path—it was a tool for transformation. My story, and my voice, mattered. Speaking Spanish wasn't just a skill; it was a superpower.

It was in that small classroom filled with other determined people—immigrants, single parents, women of color—that I found myself again. That realization ignited a fire in me. I began to see entrepreneurship not only as a way to build businesses, but as workforce development—a way to equip people with skills, confidence, and pathways to economic mobility. My own entrepreneurial journey gave me the belief in myself that I now work every day to pass on to others. It's not just my job; it's my life.

My goals were simple at first: get back on my feet, provide for my family, find stability. But those goals evolved as I grew. I didn't just want to survive, I wanted to thrive. I wanted to create opportunities not just for myself, but for others who felt invisible or left out of the traditional systems. I wanted to challenge the narrative that said women like me had to stay quiet, grateful, or small.

The tools I used? Community. Storytelling. Courage. I leaned into my lived experience and bilingual identity. I embraced public speaking even when my voice shook. I built programs to help other first-time entrepreneurs, especially those navigating language barriers and systemic inequities. I stopped waiting for permission.

There wasn't one transformational moment in my professional career. There were dozens:

- Saying yes to that first class

- Saying yes to teaching

- Saying yes to moving to St. Louis in 2016 with my new husband, Victor

- Saying yes when I was asked to become the business counselor at the Hispanic Chamber

- Saying yes to joining the BALSA Foundation and Cortex, where I now help accelerate inclusive economic growth

But the most powerful transformation came through loss.

In 2020, my son Edward passed away unexpectedly. Losing him shook me to the core. Then, in 2021, I lost my daughter Marcela. I felt broken. Wishing, hoping, wanting to believe it could not be true. No business class prepares you for that. Nothing makes it okay, and grief changes you at a cellular level, too. It makes you see the fragility of life in every sunrise, every laugh, every silence. It strips away the unimportant. It reminds you that we don't get to keep anyone forever, no matter how much we love them. And our own mortality also becomes very fragile.

Even in the pain, I chose to keep moving. I was training for the Chicago Marathon with Girls on the Run, and even though many thought I would not run it, I crossed the finish line tired and overwhelmed.

Through it all, I've come to believe that our mess can become our message—but only if we're brave enough to share it. That's what I do now. I help women find their voice. I created *Latinas Rising* with my friend and cofounder Esmeralda. Our first anthology, *Calladitas Rising,* is a #1 International Best Seller, and we are currently finalizing our second anthology, *Amigas Rising*, amplifying stories of collaboration and rising together.

When I speak to other women, I want to inspire them and wish they could see themselves through my eyes, the way I see them. They know what it's like to be underestimated. They know the exhaustion of carrying their dreams and their family's dreams at the same time. This is where my voice lives now—in the spaces where women are reclaiming their stories, building their futures, and refusing to be silent.

If I could offer one piece of advice to my past self, it would be this: You are not too late, too old, too broken, or too much. Your voice matters. Your lived experience is your strength. The things you're hiding or ashamed of? Those are the things that will connect you to others. Don't wait to be perfect to begin. Begin now.

And to the women reading this: If you feel like you're in the middle of your reinvention, trust that you're not lost. You're being rerouted. The world doesn't need more polished professionals. It needs more real women doing brave things while still figuring it out.

You don't need a cape to be a heroine. You just need to say yes to the next right thing—and keep going. And when you get stuck, ask for help!

Gabriela's journey, from Mexico to the United States, has been deeply influenced by her immigrant experience. Returning to St. Louis in 2016, Gabriela embarked on a mission to uplift small businesses, foster economic growth, and ensure language access. Her work at Cortex and the BALSA Foundation reflects her dedication to empowering entrepreneurs in underserved communities and building strong local business relationships. Her impact has been recognized with honors as a Diverse Business Leader, a Woman of Distinction, an Influential Business Woman, and a Woman of Achievement.

Gabriela's passion for elevating bilingual Latinx voices led to the creation of the Auténtico Podcast and We Live Here Auténtico, platforms that amplify stories and inspire others. Through her work, including co-founding STL Juntos during the pandemic and Latinas Rising in 2024, Gabriela honors her children, Adriana, Marcela, and Edward, who drive her work to create a better world.

Please scan the QR code to connect with this author.

**Elaine Damschen**

# Not "Or", but "And":
# The Revelation That Set Me Free

I stared at my husband. Hearing the doctor's pre-diagnosis, stark fear overtook my body. Immediately, I mentally spiraled. *God, I don't know what multiple sclerosis is. It sounds scary and horrible. My job alone isn't enough to support our family. What if Todd can't run the company anymore? How will we make an income?* My heart writhed in fear for the next several days, as my mind worried over this pile of what-if bones.

Even before the official diagnosis, I knew I must finally follow through with the leap of faith Todd had encouraged me to do. In 2001, after three years of dividing my time and energy between a bank job and mothering our children, I joined Todd full-time in what had been his venture: Mainstream Electric.

*Facing the healthcare journey ahead, how can I continue as a halftime-at-home mom when I'm a healthy, capable woman? My husband needs me!* I couldn't ignore his requests for help any longer. With our twins in kindergarten, I enrolled our eighteen-month-old in childcare.

A CT scan confirmed that some of Todd's nerves were exposed and misfiring. No doubt now, he had MS.

Over the ensuing months, Todd chose natural approaches to his health care over prescription medications. Physical activity kept his symptoms at bay, and together we took on activities like triathlon training, which reduced his muscle pain.

Our business grew fast and furiously, month after month. With no budget wiggle room to hire employees yet, Todd completed all our jobs. The frontline work of Mainstream remained a one-man show, while I took care of back-end logistics. My number one work goal was to keep stress off his nervous system. I answered the phones and dispatched 24/7. I learned the books, too.

As a former middle school teacher, I didn't know much about business, so I sought counsel at the Small Business Development Center and enrolled in classes through a local Workforce Training Center. I became a reading machine to take in all I could.

Mom-guilt ate away at me, hard. But my innate desire to "go all in" motivated me in this new role, despite how it took me away from my babies and any semblance of a social life. Other choices beyond the roles of business manager and working mama seemed past all hope. I felt trapped with no options and lived in fear of the alternative: a sick husband and no money to make the house payment or feed or clothe the littles.

I had to keep going. There was no other option. I buckled down; I hardened myself, numbing my heart. And inside, an inner light started to die. Silently, I mourned the life that *should have* been, attending the dismal burial entirely alone.

The swift death of "Elaine, half-time stay-at-home mom" set the scene for the birth of "Elaine, full-time workhorse."

My mantra became: *a business can only be as successful as its owners' limiting beliefs*. I pushed myself to the depth and breadth of my capacity. Earlier to rise and later to bed, weary and exhausted, my soul reflected the darkness of a long winter. I felt alone with my anger and bitterness about the busyness that now enslaved me.

With a new season, I heard again that the birds chirped. I felt sunlight kissing my skin, and a desire to seek something new filled my heart.

* * *

"What did you come to discuss with me today?" the psychic at the Holistic Arts Festival asked and then laughed. "I think I already know!"

I wasn't prepared for this question because my attendance at this sort of event was completely out of character for me. I didn't know what to expect. The idea that I might gain enlightenment from the gifted individuals spread across the expo hall took me by surprise. Gifted individuals... as in individuals with The Gift.

I shifted in my chair, reaching to find a really good question, the *right* question to ask. With my gaze on my lap, I explained my situation, my conflict with myself. "I am a working mom in my husband's business. I want to be a stay-at-home mom. Is that anywhere in my near future?"

The psychic looked up to the ceiling as if to consult with "our guides," or at least mine, who she affirmed were with us. After some agreeable nodding and a few "Uh, okays," she leaned forward and took both of my hands in hers and then snickered again.

"Elaine. You say you want to be a stay-at-home mother. The 'guides' tell me you are far too talented. You have too much to offer this world."

Staring at her, I angrily blurted out that when my husband and I were dating, he told me his children would never be in childcare, and his wife would be a stay-at-home mom.

Tension filled my limbs as I ground my teeth. I'd had this same conversation in my head for months, so it wasn't hard to say aloud. I added, "Because my husband was recently diagnosed with multiple sclerosis, I have to work to help him. His expectation for his wife's role came with the promise of being the wage earner, supporting the wife and children. I willingly stepped into my end of that two-way commitment. He has now become unable to keep his promise."

I knew she saw disappointment on my face. The woman continued with a firmness that surprised me. She was not snickering anymore. "You say to yourself, *I can be a working mom OR a stay-at-home mom.* Like it's one or the other. I am here to ask you, why can't you be both?"

Confused, I remained quiet. *Why did I stop at this quack's booth? She's not making any sense.*

She continued, "Elaine, you are an entrepreneur AND a mom. You are a wife AND a business partner." The "quack" assertively explained, "Replace *or* with *and*, and see how life magically changes."

Refocusing from my anger and dismissal, I replayed her words in my mind. *I am an entrepreneur AND a mother AND a wife. It's not this "or" that; it's "AND!"*

An intuitive knowing shot through my entire body as this Aha! moment bubbled to the surface. I slowly nodded my understanding, and the redhead across from me flashed another knowing grin. *This* was the reason I'd felt drawn to the holistic festival. For years, I had wanted a breakthrough, something to help me feel that I could breathe, that I wasn't failing my husband, my kids, my parents, or myself.

I suddenly knew those "*Or's*" created my mental limit. I experienced an awakening, a transformation of my entire being. For the first time, I realized my freedom.

I didn't have to miss a single thing. I could do it all: be a working mom, volunteer in the kids' classrooms, bake treats, travel, and say *yes* to all the opportunities that came my way. I walked into the rest of that day as if I'd sprouted wings. My world expanded to a new horizon.

* * *

Filled with gratitude and feeling tears well up in my eyes, I stood beneath my larger-than-life photo displayed on the Nasdaq billboard in New York City's Times Square. The International Association of Top Professionals (IAOTP) had selected me as a 2021 Top Entrepreneur of the Year for my commitment and longevity in a male-dominated industry.

While cameras flashed from all directions, time stood still, and my mind got lost, reflecting on my career in the skilled trades. *I grew Mainstream Electric, Heating, Cooling, and Plumbing from Todd and me to a team of nearly one hundred employees. We have transformed this company from nothing into a multi-million-dollar organization with thousands of satisfied clients.*

The road from that terrifying diagnosis to this Times Square celebration of success wound through some amazing experiences. Because of my passion for providing outstanding customer service, I served on the Better Business Bureau Great West and Pacific board of directors for nine years. This organization encompasses nine western U.S. states, and I helped expand its mission: to advance marketplace trust and connect consumers with businesses they can trust.

I also participated on a national board of directors called Nexstar Network. During my five years there, I contributed "to turn the world's best tradespeople into the world's best businesspeople." I met many mentors and best friends there and learned a ton.

My greatest accomplishments, though, were raising my three children. Hunter and Rhett joined Todd and me at our company as journeymen plumbers, and Emily earned her accounting degree. She too worked alongside Todd, me, and her brothers.

Todd had walked that whole path with me, surviving a few years of naturopathic treatment and enjoying ten more years symptom-free. With a passionate kiss on the lips, he then slid his arm around me for a quick snapshot. As I leaned my head on his shoulder, he whispered, "I am so proud of you."

I know my younger self would also be proud of me for persevering and becoming the woman I am today. If there is one piece of advice that I would give my younger self, or any woman who might find themselves in my situation, it would be to live by this Marianne Williamson quote. "Our deepest fear is not that we are inadequate. Our deepest fear is that we are powerful beyond measure. It is our light, not our darkness, that most frightens us. We ask ourselves, Who am I to be brilliant, gorgeous, talented, and fabulous? Actually, who are you not to be? You are a child of God. Your playing small does not serve the world. There's nothing enlightened about shrinking so that other people won't feel insecure around you. We were born to make manifest the glory of God that is within us. It's not just in some of us; it's in everyone. And as we let our own light shine, we unconsciously give other people permission to do the same. As we are liberated from our own fear, our presence automatically liberates others."

Williamson's words reflect the inner turmoil that too many women face—they might feel stretched as a wife, mother, homemaker, grocery shopper, cook, and volunteer, or experience guilt for daring to work in a career outside of the home. I find inspiration in her message that to liberate ourselves from fear, we must 'let our own light shine.' I was afraid to do this when I was younger, but now I willingly embrace it. I hope every woman can learn to do this and not place limitations on themselves. You are allowed to be brilliant, gorgeous, talented, and fabulous. Claim it!

In 2000, Elaine Damschen co-founded Mainstream Electric Heating, Cooling & Plumbing in Spokane, Washington. In 2018, 2019, and 2021, Mainstream was named to the Inc. 5000 List, which highlights the fastest-growing privately held companies in the United States. Mainstream served thousands of clients before Elaine retired from the skilled trades. With more than two decades as an entrepreneur, Damschen was named "Woman of the Year" by the *Spokesman Review* and the *Idaho Business Review*. Also named as "Top Entrepreneur of the Year" by the IAOTP, Elaine is a board member of Mountain States Policy Center and a former board member of both Nexstar Network and Better Business Bureau of the Great West and Pacific. She holds a BA in Elementary Education and an Executive MBA, both from Boise State University. Elaine has been married for more than thirty years and enjoys spending time with her daughter, twin sons, daughters-in-law, and grandchildren.

Please scan the QR code to connect with this author.

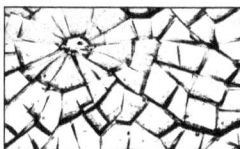

**Sheila Burkett**

# I Don't Want to Go to Jail!

The scorching heat of St. Louis in July paled in comparison to the firestorm going on inside me. An Internal Revenue Service (IRS) agent, Steve, arrived at my office, unannounced, his expression unreadable. He needed to talk to me about our unpaid payroll tax payments. I knew we were behind, but catching up on payments came second to making sure I paid all employees. Steve handed me a letter, its words striking like a gavel: Failure to send payroll taxes on time is a felony. My face flushed as panic took hold. I couldn't go to jail!

How had I let our financial situation spiral so far out of control? What would I tell my business partners? How do I explain my failure to my husband? I felt the walls closing in on me; nowhere to escape or hide…I live by a code and make decisions I can defend in a court of law. Isn't that simple? Evaluate the risks, the law, and the rules; then do what you can defend. I knew that our payroll taxes should be paid in a timely manner, but I had decided to delay the payments and preserve our cash.

IRS agent Steve sat with me in the conference room. I answered calmly and directly as we reviewed why the payments were not made, how much cash we had on hand, and our overall financial health. He asked many questions about our payroll process. Then we reviewed the consequences: the penalties to be applied. Terrified on the inside and my hands trembling under the table, I maintained eye contact and forced my voice to stay calm.

Before this incident, I knew we were behind in making the payments. But I hadn't understood the seriousness of the situation. Now that I did, I had no choice; I needed to act fast. After Steve left, I put on my "crisis hat" and jumped into action. First, I huddled with my assistant, Lisa, who handled payroll and our tax payments. She had a well-organized file of our late notices along with a spreadsheet that tracked everything we owed.

Lisa was also highly stressed about the situation. Although not an owner of the company, she was my friend. I hadn't realized how much our financial situation weighed heavily on her.

Next, I told my business partners. They had thought we were through the worst of it, and I had protected them from the full details. New to business and still learning to understand profit & loss statements, they trusted me to manage the finances.

Shame swept over me, a tidal wave that seemed to pull my breath out of my body. As I shared the story of the IRS agent coming to our office and my plan to pay our balance, penalties, and interest, they were relieved to hear a solid plan. Yet, they were also learning that I hadn't been transparent earlier. Trust was broken by this new view of reality.

That evening, the hardest discussion happened with my husband. Needless to say, he was not happy that I had put our home, our savings, and myself at risk. I told him that I had sold some of my 401(k) to cover payroll and expenses for the company. Although he was angry about the situation, he reassured me that they wouldn't haul me off to jail if I paid it off. Once again, trust was broken, but I was determined to earn it back.

How did I get here? I was a law-abiding citizen. I paid my taxes proudly and understood their importance. The reality of the situation was that this was the result of a major setback in our company the year before. Our largest client had cut their contract agreement because they had run out of funding. Due to the 2012 election, we had two additional contracts cancelled as the clients were concerned about the economy. We went from a great year to a terrible year in less than a few weeks. It was our first major crisis as a company, and we weren't sure how we would survive.

At the time, there were four founders plus a handful of employees. The founders took a significant pay cut so we could grow the business. As we discussed cutting the founders' pay even further, it was too much for one of our owners. She decided it was time for her to move and to leave Spry Digital. It was hard for us as a team, but the right thing for her. To compensate for this loss, I took over her responsibilities while still doing my original duties.

One of the major blunders during this time was our reluctance to lay off or terminate staff. Looking back today, it is amazing how we remained in business. We lived paycheck to paycheck as a business. We always held terms net 30 and had great processes to keep up on getting paid. Getting cash in the door was a priority, and at times, getting that $500 payment was the difference between having enough cash to pay our bills. Still to this day, we have a low accounts receivable and few late payments due to the processes we developed in 2013. No matter what, the owners' unwillingness to reduce staff in a timely manner was due to a lack of financial transparency.

As cash became tight, I held off making some of our payroll tax payments and our Simple IRA contributions. It was a short period of time, but playing catch-up while maintaining our current payments was difficult. I had loaned money to the company to cover payroll without telling my husband or my business partners. Day after day, it was a juggling act of keeping clients happy and the business running.

2013 is also when we moved into a renovated space that we committed to in 2012. It was a building that my husband and I owned separately from Spry Digital and Tuxedo Park Leasing. The renovation was completed in

August 2013. This created additional expenses, including new furniture, increased rent, and, of course, an open house for the new space. One decision after another compounded on top of each other. Each one added to the financial stress on the business and on me personally.

Our revenue in 2013 was approximately 41% less than it was in 2012. We went into 2014 full of energy, and it resulted in growing our revenue by 45% that year. We continued that revenue growth until 2022. In 2021 and 2022, we were recognized as one of the Inc. 5000 Fastest Growing companies.

Having an IRS agent show up at my door seems so long ago, and it was over such a small amount of money! As I reflect on what I learned from this experience, there were so many lessons I still rely on today.

The first lesson is to make reductions before you get into trouble. If the pandemic has taught us anything, it is how life is unpredictable and there are things you cannot control. No matter what you do, you may be faced with a reduction in revenue. Managing cash flow, monitoring leading indicators, and reviewing your budget will help you see when you need to make decisions. Then make them. The sooner you can let your team know what is happening, the better off everyone will be. If you are managing in fear and stress, it shows and can impact your team.

The next lesson that Debi Corrie, who is the founder of Acumaxum, a business consulting firm, taught me is that it is critical to maintain working capital. Working capital is the difference between your current assets (money or cash in the bank and accounts receivable for most of us) and current liabilities (bills or loans that must be paid within a year). You can quickly get into financial trouble if you carry too much debt. As a service business, most of our monthly expenses are payroll; the balancing act is to make sure you have enough money in the bank to cover your monthly expenses when a client may pay late. If your typical payment terms with clients are net 30 (they pay in 30 days), then you must have at a minimum 30 days of positive working capital. I have been told the goal should be to have six months of operating expenses in working capital available. It is a goal Spry Digital keeps working toward. My leaders understand what happens if you don't have enough working capital and how hard it is to rebuild.

In the service industry, maintaining a low average collection period or a low aging accounts receivable balance is very helpful. Our collections process plays a key role in our finance department. We have a well-documented process along with a documented standard operating procedure. Our team is cross-trained in case the primary person responsible for collections is out. The expectation internally and with our clients is that our preferred payment methodology is an ACH payment setup for recurring payments.

The last lesson I learned from my experience with the IRS is to trust your partners, leaders, and significant others when you are facing issues that impact your financial situation. Carrying that burden alone is exhausting, can destroy relationships, and is not an effective way to creatively solve the problems at hand. We build trust through open communication and discussing tough issues before they become monumental problems.

As a company that operates on the Entrepreneurial Operating System (EOS), we have leading indicators in our scorecard to make sure everyone understands how much cash is in the bank and what our working capital is on a weekly basis. I also delegated the day-to-day management of our finance and accounting area. We outsourced our bookkeeping function to bring additional, independent reporting to the leadership team. Our entire team knows how we are doing financially and has access to how we are operating against our budget. I also keep my husband updated on how things are going. Each of these strategies has strengthened our company, improved the trust in our ownership team, and ensured my husband isn't surprised.

As I look back on the day when the IRS agent showed up at our office, I am grateful that I had the ability to keep myself and the company out of serious trouble. Since I was able to make the outstanding payments quickly, we only had to pay a penalty and fines. I was spared any public embarrassment or injunctions. And, most importantly, I did not go to jail!

Only a few people know about this situation. The shame I felt at the time was heavy, and I sometimes wonder whether I should share this story at all. Ultimately, I decided to share this story because of the positive impact it had on my management skills and how Spry Digital operates our company. I still lead with empathy and putting our people first. The one change we made is that if we don't stay financially viable, Spry Digital will fail to exist. Celebrating 15 years of being in business in 2025 makes 2013 the distant past, where we grew so that we could navigate bigger obstacles.

Sheila Burkett, co-founder and CEO of Spry Digital, is a networker, mentor, and community leader. Her passion is helping women and people of color succeed in technology, both in business and as humans.

Driven by her entrepreneurial spirit and technology experience, Sheila started Spry Digital in April 2010. Spry Digital helps organizations reach their full potential through the design and development of high-quality websites, web apps, and brand identities that enable growth.

Sheila has a bachelor's degree from the University of Missouri-St. Louis and an MBA from Washington University in St. Louis. She serves on the Kirkwood Human Rights Commission and the COBA Dean Advisory Board at UMSL. She received a 2023 and 2024 St. Louis Titan 100 award and a 2022 YWCA Leader of Distinction award. She is also a contributing author of the *Growth—Deconstructing GRIT Collection*. In her free time, Sheila enjoys reading, gardening, and shopping for antiques.

Please scan the QR code to connect with this author.

**Tara Kinney**

# Surviving the School of Hard Knocks

Memories of my life as a toddler have been regaled at dinner tables and family events as long as I can remember. My baby book is full of sticky notes and journal entries about my entrepreneurial escapades. If the stories are accurate, my first adventure in business occurred at age three when I washed gravel in the dog water bowl and sold it door-to-door. My parents found me on the neighbor's doorstep with one pocket full of gravel and another full of nickels.

Scrapbooked evidence of successful and failed business attempts is documented alongside accounts of my stealthy escapes from home, my rough and tumble injuries, and my emotional outbursts of authoritarianism. I was a brave and determined child, strong-willed, always pushing or ignoring boundaries, plotting and planning the next great idea, demanding attention, and taking control in every group setting with an empathetic heart. This might very well be the way people describe me today as a business owner, board member, executive leader, teammate, volleyball coach, mother, and wife.

## "When I Grow Up"—Adult Reality Rooted in Childhood Dreams

As a parent, the traits that defined me sound a lot like the description of a nightmare child. In retrospect, we could say that I was honing my confidence to explore opportunities, persevere through setbacks, try new things, and overcome obstacles.

In this context, it makes perfect sense that my childhood career aspirations ranged from the Queen of California or a tomb raiding archaeologist, or an adventuring conservationist like Dian Fossey, saving whatever is in danger. These career ambitions exactly match the core characteristics that I have fought to retain and leverage my entire life—leader, explorer, savior.

Throughout school, college, career, and entrepreneurship, strong forces try to endanger whatever I try to save, destroy whatever I try to discover, and take my "Queen" title, so I submit to their control. This is the school of hard knocks, and I will confidently continue to explore, persevere, and overcome obstacles as I grow up. Suddenly, all those traits that were once perceived as negative can be reframed as strengths in the school of hard knocks. Brave, strong-willed, boundary-breaking, attention-seeking, empathetic, visionary, boss—yep, that's me!

## Knowing Your Value Despite Other Opinions

Half the battles in the school of hard knocks are complicated by the perceptions of others that make us doubt ourselves. Clarity around what you value about yourself will help you maintain confidence regardless of societal norms, other opinions, and imposed boundaries that suck your joy and limit your potential.

While my neighbors did not necessarily value gravel, they did value the buying experience. At the time, my parents did not value my bold confidence and adventurous spirit, but all the adults in that rock-peddling-toddler story valued my idea and my effort. What did I value? Who knows, I was three! Maybe I valued improving the gravel by washing it. I probably valued earning my own money. And knowing myself, I definitely valued the independence. Despite getting in trouble, this experience solidified my confidence in myself. It did not hurt to get in trouble, and by asking for forgiveness instead of permission, I was rewarded with a pocket full of nickels. These foundational childhood lessons have served me well in the school of hard knocks as a businessperson.

In our first jobs, we are conditioned to believe that working long hours, caving to the demands of others, and being subservient to tenured team members provides a path to promotion. It quickly became obvious that good work earns you more work, while others slack off and get rewarded with smaller or easier assignments. Then you realize that everyone gets bonuses and raises regardless of how much they work; promotions are often based on tenure, not performance; and respect is earned when you demand it, not when you deserve it.

For example, I value my strong work ethic, which is something that others also seem to appreciate. However, in the marketing and business development department (cost center), you are "of service" to the engineers (profit center) in an A/E/C professional services firm. The business culture, professional advancement pathways, and compensation plans often devalue the contributions of non-engineering business functions. This culture complicates the project management of business development initiatives where engineer contributions to proposals and scopes of work are required to meet precise deadlines. In the school of hard knocks, someone said, "You should be grateful that the engineers prioritize their billable work so you have a job," to which I immediately responded, "You should be grateful I do business development so your engineers have billable work and a job to do." Bold move. Respect earned.

While my more experienced peers were shocked by my candor, no one could argue with that young professional woman defending her value in a male-dominated field where tenured engineers called the shots. After the resulting promotion, my confidence in my value solidified. Yet, the 20+ hour workdays continued because respect and promotion did not change a business culture that punished my relentless get-it-done, make-it-happen tenacity with more work. So many businesses set themselves up to fail top performers, and many top performers stop delivering value as a result. This lesson has been pivotal to surviving the school of hard knocks as a business leader.

## Confidence to Succeed Without Fearing the Unknown

When I was recruited to help start a new business, I confidently left that job in a beautiful urban high-rise to accept the uncertainty of a non-traditional role in a business that didn't yet exist. It was both bold and brave to leave a coveted job with a reputable company to be a part-time contractor with a laptop on a couch. In 2005, virtual work was done with flip phones and fax machines, but securing clients to grow a business, building brand, systems, tools, and teams from scratch is the same regardless of your tech stack.

Looking back, that part-time contractor with a laptop on a couch has turned into a businesswoman with multiple fractional executive roles on more than 45 leadership teams to date. That brave first step into the unknown has led to rewarding clarity of my value, giving me the confidence to build businesses with big risks and hard work. Self-sufficient, independent, strong-willed—those same values honed as a child continue to carry me through many lessons in business, entrepreneurship, and customer success.

While my intrinsic value has not changed much over decades of professional experience, my confidence has evolved with a greater understanding and recognition of how others perceive my value. Even when we strive for the same end goal, our priorities, expectations, or motivations can differ quite drastically.

Appreciating and recognizing the value of others used to compel me to question my value and conform to their demands, spawning questions of uncertainty and self-doubt. Over the past 20 years, I have witnessed how other entrepreneurs and business leaders experience this same challenge. While some withstand the pressure, others cave to follow a dark path toward delusional and unreputable versions of success that never satisfy their needs or fulfill their ambitions. In hindsight, it has become clear that "fear of the unknown" causes people to make irrational choices, lose their confidence, and deviate from their values. However, as founders, we must boldly go where others have never been, taking risks that others would never take, and losing as often as we win.

Discovering what is possible requires trying new things, trusting yourself to solve challenges along the journey, and maintaining confidence despite the setbacks and disappointments. My greatest challenges have stemmed from decisions made when I was unconfident and fearing the unknown. Overcoming those self-inflicted lessons in the school of hard knocks will take years of rebuilding confidence and reinforcing values.

## Education is Expensive, and Time is Money

The best lessons are learned when overcoming great losses. Business failures teach more than successes, but those lessons are expensive, and time is more valuable than money. For most business owners, the first 10-20 years as an entrepreneur present a series of grueling, exhausting, and intensely complex challenges during which we are expected to look glamorous, appear excited, and sugar-coat the experience. Well, that's b*llsh*t!

While my first experience in entrepreneurship was in building someone else's business, I saw the good, the bad, and the ugly second-hand. And I saw an opportunity to make a business out of my passion and experience building businesses. In my first business, I learned some valuable and expensive lessons that prepared me for even harder challenges and more expensive lessons in the businesses that followed.

As that first business got tough to run and grow by myself, imposter syndrome set in as all these other founders and business owners maintained a façade of fake confidence, false success, and rented glamour. Fear of the unknown and lack of self-confidence led me to believe that the challenges existed because I was in business alone. I told myself that someone with more and different experience must be necessary to scale my business. In pursuit of collaboration and shared risk, I set myself up for the most expensive lesson of my 25-year career.

If you only learn one lesson vicariously through my experience, please let it be that choosing the wrong business partner(s) costs entrepreneurs more irreparable damage than the risk of business ownership. From loss of time to loss of money to loss of confidence and loss of clarity— ownership transitions have been the most expensive lessons in the school of hard knocks.

As my business enters its 10th year, it is the first year that I own 100% of the company. While I now officially carry all the burden and all the risk, my workload and business contributions did not change with or without shared ownership. My team still shares the lessons of perseverance as we collaborate toward shared objectives, appreciating everyone's value, and building a shared future with clarity and confidence.

## Rebuilding Confidence and Clarity in Pursuit of "Happily Ever After"

While my value will never be enough for some and may be considered "overvalued" to others, the school of hard knocks has taught me that you will never please everyone. Exploring opportunities where your value aligns for mutual benefit on a journey toward a shared goal allows us to maintain clarity and confidence without falling victim to the perception of value that others try to force upon us. We will compromise, we will negotiate, but we will do so while remaining true to what we value so that we do not lose confidence in the school of hard knocks.

Maintaining clarity around what I value within the context of what others value is the difference between a "good queen" and a "bad queen." Prioritizing my value to my family, my value to my team, my value to my clients, and my value to my community, while staying true to who I am as a leader, is exactly the kind of queen I imagined. Even our most childish aspirations, like "becoming the Queen of California," can guide our confidence to make decisions, learn lessons, and pursue opportunities. We hire employees who make commitments, select vendors who make promises, and join partners to share burdens.

At the end of the day, business success is a series of day-by-day, play-by-play decisions informed by and made within the school of hard knocks. While those without entrepreneurial experience might believe this life is full of glamorous, exhilarating, world-shattering adventures, many of us are focused on surviving the school of hard knocks without losing what we value in the pursuit of ambitious visions.

As much as parents, teachers, coaches, peers, and colleagues have found my innate characteristics challenging, they learn to respect and appreciate those same traits when it comes to accomplishing outcomes. People often try to change us, quiet us, and hold us to their standards. By resisting those pressures, we can find inner strength, confidence, and clarity about who we are and what is truly most important to us.

I believe that the people who are truly happy with their life and proud of their achievements are those who don't lose themselves trying to make others happy, or conforming to others' definition of success. Life is never long enough, work is never done enough, money will never be enough, and we can never love or be loved enough. Happiness makes us grateful that we *are* enough. Being true to ourselves makes us happy and grateful, which gives us the confidence to embrace all the good, the bad, the beautiful, and the ugly within ourselves and within others. This cycle strengthens and restores confidence that we will survive the school of hard knocks.

Tara Kinney is an international public speaker, Fractional CRO, executive board member, and business owner. While her career includes decades of creative and professional writing, Tara's first published work can be found in the *Unsung Heroines of Business* Anthology.

Tara delights audiences with a fresh and snarky perspective that highlights parallels between human development and business lifecycles. As a business professional, youth volleyball coach, wife, and mother, she has heard all the excuses. She thrives on finding similarities between people of any age and businesses of all sizes. She writes from a place of experience, humor, compassion, and acceptance of the messiness that is human life. Tara kindly reminds us that we aren't special, and our businesses aren't unique, but our professional experience and business size can certainly exacerbate the same messes we have been making since infancy or start-up—it's human nature.

Please scan the QR code to connect with this author.

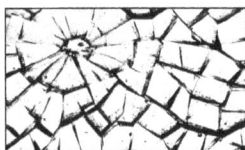

**Lusnail Rondón Haberberger**

# From Bad to Good: The LUZCO Journey

## The Spark

I didn't set out to become a CEO. The entrepreneurial flame was first lit during my MBA at UCLA. Surrounded by visionaries and thinkers, I began to imagine a future where I could lead something of my own. But it wasn't until my boys were born that the fire truly caught. I realized that I needed balance—a place where I could be professionally challenged without sacrificing the joy of being a mom. I needed a change. I needed to build a life filled with "both ands" instead of "either ors." I needed…to start my own business?

LUZCO was born from that need. It is a company born not just from strategy, but from the soul. The company was a combination of my ambition, dedication to motherhood, and a deep desire to build something meaningful. We were a tiny team at the start—scrappy, passionate, and wildly unprepared. We often joked that we were "building the plane as we were flying it." And it was true. We had no operating procedures, no job descriptions, no onboarding process. We just did what needed to be done—for our clients, team, and partners.

One of my colleagues once joked that while some companies go from "good to great," we were going from "bad to good." It stuck. Not because we were truly bad, but because we were inexperienced. We didn't know what we didn't know. And that was okay! Most successful entrepreneurs do not know what they are doing at the beginning. They have a solution to a problem and try to monetize that, and along the way, they make mistakes—mistakes that ultimately become the best teachers.

## Torn Between Two Worlds

Before founding LUZCO, I spent years immersed in the electric utility industry. After graduating with a degree in electrical engineering, I began my career in the field—literally. I visited substations, climbed into manholes, and surveyed power lines to design replacements for aging copper communication systems, transitioning them to modern fiber optic networks. It was hands-on, technical, and deeply fulfilling.

As my career progressed, I transitioned into project management, leading increasingly complex, multimillion-dollar initiatives. With each new challenge, my confidence and capabilities grew. But so did my responsibilities at home. Both of my sons, José and Luca, were born during this time. Balancing the nurturing demands of motherhood with the high-stakes pressure of managing large-scale infrastructure projects was exhausting—and enlightening.

I knew I wanted something different. Something that honored both my professional ambition and my personal values. But the turning point came when I was told I couldn't be considered for a promotion because I had taken two maternity leaves in three years. That moment shattered me. It was clear that the workplace didn't see me as the engineer or project manager I was. They saw me as just a mom.

So, I decided to build something different...my own version of balance and success. LUZCO became the space where I could be a leader and a mother, a visionary and a nurturer. It was time to stop choosing between two worlds and start creating one where both could thrive.

# From Bad to Good

But where do I start? I considered myself an excellent project manager, so I targeted my clients (electric utilities) to provide that service. I was fortunate to obtain a contract to manage Electrical Transmission projects, but since I did not have any staff, my time was dedicated to delivering to the client. I was so ingrained in performing that I forgot a few key components to successfully run a business. Take invoicing, for example. In our early days, my father-in-law, whom I lovingly call Dad, was our unofficial CFO. A retired finance executive, he was also our line of credit. After three months, he asked, "Lus, I know you're working on projects, but how come we haven't seen any cash in?" I blinked. "Oh…I guess we get paid after we submit an invoice!" We hadn't sent a single invoice. We were 90 days behind in cash flow. That day, I learned one of the most important lessons in business: cash is king—or maybe queen.

That was bad. But we made it good.

Hiring was another adventure. Just like our initial capital, our first hires were friends and family. We didn't have job titles or descriptions. We just needed people who were hungry, smart, and willing to grind. They were warriors. The hiring process? Not so much. It consisted of recruiting friends and family and convincing them that it would be an exciting journey. I don't know how I was able to energize them, but I did! At the end of that first year, we grew from a company of one to five.

Over the past eight years, we've transformed that chaos into a thoughtful, strategic system. We now use behavioral and cognitive assessments, structured interviews, and a "People Analyzer" to ensure alignment with our values. The People Analyzer (part of the trademark of Entrepreneurial Operating System) consists of asking the hiring team: Does the candidate "want" the job instead of "needing" the job? Do they "get" the job? (Do they understand what the role entails?) Do they have the "capacity" to do the job? Are they a cultural fit? These new strategies helped strengthen the company.

We also improved when I finally accepted that I did not have to carry the company solely on my shoulders. As an engineer, I was used to solving problems myself. But building a company taught me the power of delegation. I learned to focus on our core—what I call our "bread and butter"—and outsource the rest. Accounting, legal, banking—these became partnerships, not burdens. I found experts who could do what I couldn't, and I leaned on them.

We also implemented daily huddles, strategic planning sessions, and performance metrics inspired by books like *Good to Great* and *Built to Last*. But our real transformation came from embracing our own version of those principles, customized for who we are and what we value: leadership, familia (family), and diversity.

LUZCO isn't just a company. It's a reflection of my journey, my values, and my belief that business can be both profitable and personal. We've built a culture where authenticity is celebrated, where people can show up as their whole selves, and where growth is measured not just in revenue, but in resilience.

We've faced challenges: economic downturns, industry shifts, and internal growing pains. But each obstacle became an opportunity to refine, to learn, and to lead with intention.

## From Good to Great: The Next Chapter

Today, LUZCO is no longer the scrappy startup it once was. We're a thriving, values-driven organization with a clear mission and a strong foundation. But we never forget where we came from. We honor our "bad to good" journey because it keeps us humble, hungry, and human.

I often tell my team: We're not just building a company—we're building a legacy. One that our children can be proud of. One that proves you don't have to choose between being a great parent and a great leader. One that shows that with courage, community, and a little bit of chaos, you can turn anything from bad to good.

Now, we're entering a new phase—moving from good to great. This journey is different. It's more strategic, more intentional, and still full of learning curves. But the foundation is stronger. We've built systems, culture, and clarity. We've learned to measure what matters and to invest in what lasts.

And yet, the heart of our journey remains the same: growth through grit.

## A Message to My Fellow Heroines

To every woman reading this who's building something—whether it's a business, a dream, or a life—know this: Your struggles do not define you. They shape you. They strengthen you. They teach you.

The path from bad to good, and from good to great, is paved with obstacles. But each one is a stepping stone. Each mistake is a lesson. Each challenge is a chance to rise.

Don't give up. Don't shrink yourself. Don't wait for permission. Instead, you must build your plane, fly it, and learn as you go.

And if you're just starting out, here's my biggest piece of tactical advice: Hire a great accountant, find a trustworthy bank, and employ an awesome lawyer. These partners will be your lifeline. They'll help you stay afloat when the waves get rough.

But more than anything, surround yourself with people who believe in you. People who will challenge you, support you, and grow with you.

You are not alone. You are not behind. You are building something extraordinary.

And that, my dear heroine, is how you go from bad to good—and from good to great.

Lusnail Rondón Haberberger is the founder and CEO of LUZCO Technologies, LLC, "LUZCO," which she launched in 2017. Under her leadership, LUZCO grew from a one-person business into an award-winning, certified woman-owned and minority-owned boutique engineering firm, with offices in Missouri, Kansas, and New York. Lus' portfolio of awards includes: 2020 *Small Business Monthly* Top Women Business Owners Award, The *St. Louis Business Journal's* 2021 C-Suite Awards, and The *St. Louis Business Journal's* 2022 Most Influential Business Woman.

As a Venezuelan-born mother of two, Lus has made it her mission to expand resources for local youth, immigrants, and women interested in STEM careers and entrepreneurship. She participates in expert panels and mentoring programs, and launched LUZCOmmunity, a team of LUZCO employees dedicated to philanthropy. While thoroughly dedicated to her company and her community, Lus always makes time for her three favorite people: her husband, Dan, and her two boys, José and Luca.

Please scan the QR code to connect with this author.

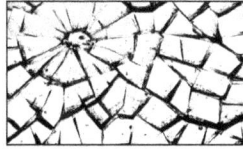

**Taryn Pulliam**

# Surviving the Winds of Change

Change is an inevitable part of life. Whether it is outgrowing a relationship, moving to a new city, or getting a promotion, change can be scary. However, it can also be transformative.

In 2024, I made a major life decision to end my marriage. For the last several years, I had been struggling with the question many of us face: *Is it better for my son to keep our family together or to go and start a life where we could find a more peaceful existence?* I was also struggling with my faith. I am a Christian, and I know the Bible teaches that divorce is not ideal. So, I was fighting an internal battle, I was losing, and it was slowly killing me.

I couldn't sleep; I was praying through the nights, trying to find a way to fix it. Walking on eggshells, barely speaking to the man I loved, who had now become a roommate who lived just downstairs, but so far away. I also reached out to a counselor to find out what we could do to fix it. You see, I don't quit, I don't give up—I make things happen. This was very unfamiliar territory to me. Sadly, I was losing; I couldn't fix it, no one could help me fix it, and I had to give up.

About six months later, the divorce was final. Getting a divorce can be one of the most heartbreaking and challenging experiences a person can go through. It signifies the end of a significant relationship, but it is also the beginning of a new chapter. The emotional turmoil can be overwhelming, but it also offers an opportunity for personal growth and self-discovery. It's a chance to redefine oneself, to learn from past experiences, and to build a future that aligns more closely with one's true values and desires.

As a result of the divorce, I felt I could not stay in my home. There was no way I could be there and heal. Everywhere I looked, there was a memory. I thought to myself, *Why does he get a fresh start, and I am stuck here with all our old stuff?* I decided I wanted to move. No, I needed to move. So, I started looking for a new place. It took me a couple of months, but I found a new home and planned to move. I began packing our four-bedroom, three-bath home. It was like a huge mountain in front of me, but on the other side, I knew there was a clean slate.

Moving to a new place is another significant change that can evoke a mix of excitement and fear. The prospect of starting fresh in a new environment can be thrilling, but it also means leaving behind the familiar and stepping into the unknown. However, this transition is another opportunity to explore new cultures, meet new people, create new memories, and recalibrate what truly matters.

Since I was essentially rebuilding my life, I decided it was time to dive back into my career goals and make sure they were accomplished. In late 2019, I started my career with GadellNet. When I started, I had a plan. I wanted to move into a leadership role to share my years of experience in sales and to help develop a team of sales professionals and truly impact the organization. Over the last five years, I have had the pleasure of working with the most incredibly talented team. I was learning more every day through ongoing training, attending thought leadership luncheons, and was able to be mentored by many brilliant leaders both inside and outside of the organization.

While this was very exciting, I began to realize that all this change came with some pressure. When I was going through these changes, I literally caught myself trying to catch my breath. I used to do a lot of yoga, and I learned that as you stretch the mind and body, you may feel pain, but if you take deep breaths, you can breathe through the pain and eventually master new poses. This time, I was trying to master a new life.

This got me thinking. Why am I breathing like this? It got me wondering, what are the most stressful life events?

Well, here they are:

1.  Death of a family member: While my ex-husband did not die, our relationship did.

2.  Divorce or separation: Check.

3.  Moving into a new home: Check.

4.  Your own sickness or the sickness of a family member: My mental health had taken a heavy toll, and I felt like I still had much to accomplish.

Wow! Within a three-month period, I had lived through all these stressors. But you know what? It was temporary. By the grace of God and my wonderful circle of friends and family, I made it. I was going to be okay.

For starters, I absolutely loved my new home. It was my dream home. It had an open-floor plan, beautiful white cabinets, quartz counters, wood floors, a fireplace, and a pool. My son now has kids who knock on our door to play with him. This never happened in our old neighborhood. I put Christmas lights up this year, and I decorated my mantle with adorable snowmen and garland, and made it our own personal wonderland.

Then I had another dream come true.

In late 2024, I was finally blessed with the opportunity that I had been working toward. I was promoted to Vice President of Strategic Services at GadellNet. I now lead a team of talented professionals whose passions align with mine—for growth and continued innovation. Now, while receiving a promotion is a positive change, it also comes with its own set of challenges. A promotion means increased responsibilities, higher expectations, and fear of the unknown. However, it also signifies recognition of one's hard work and capabilities. It's an opportunity to grow professionally, to develop new skills, and to make a significant impact within the organization.

Now you may be thinking to yourself, "Where is she going with this?" Well, I wanted to provide this insight: While change can be scary, it also brings new opportunities. Embracing change with an open mind and positive attitude can lead to personal and professional growth. It's a chance to let go of the past, to learn from experiences, and to move forward with renewed purpose and determination.

To anyone who has faced, or may be facing, a big change, whether it be personal or professional, I want to highlight a good plan to shut the door on things you may not need as you grow into the next phase of your life. I also want to provide some guidance on a plan to set up goals to thrive in the next chapter of life.

The first habit I plan to leave behind is negative self-talk. Self-criticism can be a major barrier to personal growth. I plan to practice self-compassion and positive affirmation to build a healthier mindset.

Next up is avoiding procrastination. Delaying tasks can lead to unnecessary stress and missed opportunities. I plan to embrace a proactive approach to responsibilities and goals to crush goals and soar higher.

Then, there is the need to keep it clean! Clutter can be overwhelming in your mind, in your heart, and in your work. Simplify each environment and prioritize what truly matters to create a more focused and peaceful life.

Finally, let go of toxic relationships. These can be in your personal life or at work. Surround yourself with people who uplift and support you.

Eliminate relationships or unfulfilling work environments that drain your energy and hinder your progress.

Perhaps the most important thing to do in the next chapter of your life is to create a clear plan that aligns with your values and establishes several personal and professional goals. It is crucial to define what you want to achieve in your career, for your health, and for your personal growth. Having clear goals will give you the direction and motivation needed to turn your dreams of a new chapter into a reality!

Taryn Pulliam is the vice president of strategic partnerships at GadellNet Consulting Services. She has over 25 years of experience in business and relationship development. She specializes in cultivating new relationships and finding strategic partners.

Taryn is also a board member of Covenant House Missouri. This organization helps homeless youth transition from homelessness to hope. Taryn's family and faith are at the center of what she loves most.

Please scan the QR code to connect with this author.

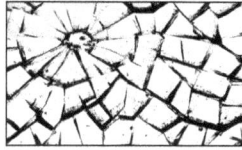

**Amy Lemire**

# Creating the Sales Confidence Code

The week started off as a typical Monday as a sales training manager for a medical device company. It was in the early months of 2020, and I had just returned home from our national sales meeting over the weekend in Orange County, California. I had planned to travel the next day with a sales representative in the field in Colorado. However, I began to feel a cold coming on, congestion, and a sore throat, and I made the decision that maybe I should stay home this week. After contacting the sales rep to cancel my travel plan, an hour later, I received an email from our human resources department. It was a warning to all employees nationwide not to travel; there were safety concerns over a new virus that was spreading globally. I assumed this would last for a week, maybe two. Little did I know what would unfold over the coming months, not only for the world, but for the next transition that would happen in my life.

2020 had already been a year of transition, after enduring a difficult and costly divorce at the beginning of 2019. Then came the sale of my house in the northwestern suburbs of Chicago, followed by a settlement that ended up costing me over $200,000. Then, in the midst of that transition, I was laid off, along with the entire leadership team of the last company I was at as a global director of sales training. The silver lining was a 6-month severance package, with full pay and benefits, that gave me the time to reset, reflect, and decide "What do I really want in my life?" I had recently been certified as a Thought Habits/Habit Finder coach, and I thought, *Maybe I could do this part-time…create coaching groups. It could be a fun hobby that would keep me from going into another corporate job and pay cash for my divorce settlement. Maybe I will live in St. Louis temporarily, and then move somewhere else.*

The "stay at home" orders went from weeks to months. After my expensive divorce and move back to my hometown, I had taken this corporate training job to get benefits and keep a sense of routine in my life after a turbulent time and months of emotional, physical, and financial transition. But I began to dream of what it would be like if I could run my own business full-time, coaching on the Thought Habits, and doing sales training as a consultant for many companies, instead of one. I was put to the test every day. Our vice president of sales and the entire sales leadership team began to worry and frantically ask, "What can we do to keep the sales team busy?" The sales team was locked out of the hospitals they were calling on due to the quarantine. The solution was to do more sales training.

At first, I thought it was a great idea. Then, my coaching groups called "The Best Version of You: Success Habits Breakthrough" began to take off. I was running a 9-week, 1-hour per week coaching group on Wednesday nights, then I started another cohort on Saturday mornings. Between my full-time job and the coaching cohorts I created, I was working about 60 hours a week. I was exhausted. I remember talking on FaceTime to my boyfriend (now my husband), Nigel, and he commented about the dark circles under my eyes. I could see that the biggest problem was not my being burned out and exhausted; it was the fact and realization that doing more tactical sales training was not the answer. The company I was working for had no idea that there was an "emotional" and mental health crisis on their hands. A team of 50 sales reps nationwide was in lockdown and under stress to meet a sales quota, despite not being able to see customers and prospects face-to-face for sales appointments.

The lightbulb moment happened. I began to see that training teams on "tactics and skills" or the "doing/outer game" is only half of the success equation. The other half is the "thought habits" or the "being/inner game" that matter. I could see my coaching clients who were working on their thought habits and their inner game in my program excelled and overcame the stress and emotional turmoil from the lockdown. On the other hand, the sales team members, who were focused on skills and doing more, remained stuck.

I also remembered that early in my sales career, my sales results skyrocketed once I began to work on my thought habits, emotions, and self-confidence. I also joined Toastmasters and attended self-development seminars every chance I could. Why were the corporations I was working for in sales—and later in my career, sales training—missing this idea of the "inner game" of mastering thought habits and self-confidence?

I saw a new vision for myself. I hired a coach and set a huge goal, a goal that seemed both scary and impossible. I wanted to quit my full-time job and start my own sales training consulting business where I could coach success "mindset" habits, in addition to sales skills and tactics. I did not know how, but I knew I had a why. I also felt my heart and intuition tell me that *everything would work out great.*

I finally mustered up the courage to tell my boss, the vice president of sales, of my plans to leave the company and fulfill my new mission of teaching. Then I gave him several months' notice. The conversation felt awkward, as I knew the idea of bringing a new focus to sales training, including "coaching on success habits," seemed foreign in the corporate world. I called this concept "The Sales Confidence Code," and it was my vision of teaching the world that we play two games in sales and success: an inner game of mindset/habits, and an outer game of tactics/action.

My last day of full-time employment was November 21, 2021. The last day of my job, I felt like I was having an out-of-body experience. I was excited and terrified all at the same time. After all, where would my first client come from? At 3 p.m., the vice president of sales contacted me and asked, "Would you consider working here part-time as a consultant?" I took a deep breath and said, "Yes!" An offer was made that was way below the fees I had in mind. We negotiated, and by 6 p.m., we had an agreement in place.

As I look back, trading my paycheck for my passion was the best decision I have made. Like my days in sales, there have been peaks and valleys, but in the end, I would not trade this for anything. Being my own boss has been the most gratifying growth experience I have ever known. Also, sharing my vision with companies, leaders, sales professionals, and entrepreneurs, and seeing them overcome the resistance, anxiety, and emotional roller coaster that the profession of selling oftentimes feels like, has been more rewarding than focusing on collecting a bi-weekly paycheck. Through mastering the inner game of thought habits, the biggest win is watching my clients win, which made my decision to leave my corporate job priceless.

Now, more than three years later, whenever I share my story, I include the message that an entrepreneurship journey is not all rainbows and unicorns! My initial financial success involved billing my former employer weekly for my consulting. I noticed that the sometimes-negative culture, lack of treating one another with respect, and internal politics took the fun out of my work and were out of alignment with my personal mission, values, and mastery of success habits. Eventually, I began to feel like an employee again.

One of my biggest lessons learned came from relying on one big corporate consulting client for my income. I spent so much time focusing on and serving the one big client that I neglected growing my client list.

Similar to my sales career, I quickly learned that sales and business development are the top priorities, and it is a daily habit.

I also struggled early in my entrepreneurial journey as I juggled servicing two markets: business-to-consumer coaching clients and business-to-business corporations seeking sales training. I failed to realize how much intentional focus, energy, and time it was taking to service both sides of my business. As one side of my business grew, the other side of the business was getting neglected, and vice versa. I had heard early and often in my career from other coaches and mentors, "pick a lane," and "niches lead to riches." But failing to follow that advice ended up costing me in many ways. Burnout and having a tough time focusing eventually affected my income. My second year in business, my revenue and cash flow became a roller coaster when I parted ways with my first big client, my former employer.

By the summer of 2024, I had increased my corporate consulting client list, and my business began to thrive once again. I had hired a part-time executive assistant, Michelle, a huge win in helping me to focus more on servicing my clients and my sales efforts of gaining new clients. I had also heard "do not wait until you are making the big bucks to hire help," and I am relieved that I have continued to follow that advice today. Not only was Michelle a huge source of support for my weekend events, virtual coaching, and consulting, but she was also a friend I had known for 15 years. I trusted her. There were many times she was a trusted advisor and sounding board, as I navigated being a new business owner, president, and CEO. However, I was unprepared for what would soon happen.

The support I had finally decided to invest in came to a screeching halt. An early August video call with my executive assistant, Michelle, turned out to be the last one with her. I will never forget the phone call I received that day in mid-August of 2024. Michelle passed away in her sleep. I could not believe the words and was overcome with shock, sadness, and disbelief as I heard the unexpected news.

Michelle had helped me build my "Best Version of You" retreat weekends and was the backbone of the events. "Why?" I asked myself, along with all the other members of Michelle's circle, who lost a dear friend, mother, supporter, and amazing human being.

The grief and depression expected after such a loss affected my mindset. Once again, my income and sales activity plummeted. I questioned myself and my business and even wondered if I should return to working for a company and receiving a bi-weekly paycheck. Little did I know that an October cruise to Greece—which I had planned back in January with another friend named Michelle—would be the perfect solution to getting unstuck and back on track. I did not realize that I had spent a good three years working hard, grinding, and 100% neglecting the idea of taking a "time out," more than the weekend or local getaways I had taken since I quit my job. My mind was criticizing me, saying, "I should be working," while my heart, soul, and husband all said, "Go, get away, have some fun!" I am glad I listened and trusted those voices.

That reset allowed me to see that I was burned out to the core. I had been trying to be everything to everyone and was getting nowhere fast. Serving individual coaching clients and keeping weekend retreats going meant that attracting more corporate consulting clients had been relegated to my spare time.

I returned from Greece with several big decisions made. First, my focus going forward is serving one mission, and one market: bringing the "Sales Confidence Code" to the audience I spent three decades with: high-performing companies and sales teams. I decided to make my sole focus corporate consulting, speaking, and sales confidence building. I also made the tough decision to retire my retreats in 2025, to give more time to corporate clients and host virtual coaching groups instead. This went back to the roots of where I started back in 2019, and back to "what was working."

What have I learned from this adventure? Or, more importantly, what can *you* learn? The answer is to allocate more time for ourselves and our self-care. We should take more time off and avoid stressing about not doing enough. We *are* enough. We owe it to ourselves to take time to rest, heal, and recharge. Doing these things will help us be better business-women in the long run. No one will want to come to us to seek help if we are exhausted and overworked. We must all follow the Sales Confidence Code and place more emphasis on just *being* instead of doing more.

Amy Lemire, CSP, DTM, collaborates with leaders and teams to simplify sales, accelerate the pipeline, elevate performance, and amplify success. She has a passion for streamlining the sometimes-complicated world of sales. Amy has trained thousands of sales and business professionals to sell more through the mastery of best practices and success habits.

After spending more than two decades in business-to-business and medical sales and training, Amy founded AIM Training and Consulting. As a certified "Habit Finder" Leadership Coach, she is the author of 2 books: *From Zero to Sales Hero* and *From Zero to Speaker Hero*.

Designated a Certified Speaking Professional (CSP) in March 2023 by the National Speakers Association (NSA), Amy is also a VISTAGE-certified speaker, a Distinguished Toastmaster (DTM), and a member of NSA. Her business, AIM Training and Consulting, was recognized in 2024 as a "Fast 50" Business in St. Louis by *Small Business Monthly Magazine*.

Please scan the QR code to connect with this author.

## Jaclyn Noroño-Rodriguez

# We Are Never Finished Goods

*We are never finished goods.* My husband continuously reminds me of this, and the longer I think about it, the more I realize how that statement is pure truth. I go back to that moment when I was pondering about what career to choose, that moment when I thought I was pinpointing what I would do for the rest of my life. I remember being scared of the many choices, scared to choose one, and then somehow doom myself. And thus, after long deliberation, I set my own conditions: No matter what I chose, the goals were to never be bored and to make a difference.

I'd like to say that I found packaging, but what really happened was that packaging found me. In packaging terms, when I started my career, I candidly did not know what type of "product" I would be, or what retail stores I would end up at, but I knew I wanted to be unique. And as time passed, I realized that if I wanted to survive and stay relevant in the market, I was going to have to transform/repackage myself. Growth has taken time and many lessons, but here are the top five I believe to be the strongest lessons learned thus far in my career.

1. Define what success means to YOU.

We all learn about success in our own ways. As we grow up, we look around our lives and the people in them to start to define what success is for us. For me, it started with both my parents being professionals, home-owners, and even business entrepreneurs. Thanks to my parents, I grew up defining goals and actively discussing how to become a better version of myself each year. I even started working by the time I was 12, teaching English to younger kids in the same institute where my mom worked, teaching the adults. I honestly did not think my life was out of the norm; to me, that *was* the way of life.

When I moved to the United States at 16 to start college, my world opened up. I was exposed to an entirely different culture, to different backgrounds, and to different ways of life. As I connected with people, I learned that some wanted similar things to what I wanted, others wanted something way different. Some people are constantly searching for different careers and/or roles, and some are content doing the exact same work/role forever. And yet, they are all perfectly happy and successful in their own ways.

After continuously learning this, I started analyzing myself with every career change, asking myself: Did I enjoy what I was doing? Was I bored? Was I making a difference? The answers to these questions dictated quite a few changes in my life. And yes, there were a few times when I somewhat reluctantly, and very nervously, made the decision to look for different job opportunities based on the answers. And it made all the difference. Above all else, we must be purposeful about reminding ourselves what type of product we are and what success means to us.

2. Progress and growth are on YOU.

Think about it, even to get around, one must gather the strength to get up and walk to the destination. One's professional career is no different; in order for it to progress, one needs to take the steps forward. To apply this idea to a practical example, if you don't do the dishes in your house, they don't get washed. My philosophy with my growth follows a similar thought process. It is up to no one but me to proactively work on my growth as a person and as a professional.

An example of this was when I worked at the bank as a teller, and I made it a point to leverage classes they had available for self-improvement. I took them when the job was slow and always made sure I was meeting my KPIs. And throughout my career, in every role I've held, I continued to actively look for ways to become a better Jaclyn. I would read books, take classes, get certifications, and go to conferences and workshops; I would soak up every opportunity for self-development. And I can tell you from experience that it has paid off each and every time. Make sure you are continuously improving your product, aka yourself. No one else will do it for you!

3. Accept constructive criticism.

We all occasionally experience that sinking feeling in our stomachs when someone offers constructive criticism. Rather than see this feedback as helpful, we misconstrue it as a threat. We meet it with the fear that we are not good enough or that we do not measure up in some way. I have experienced this gut reaction to advice aimed at helping me grow multiple times in my career. However, there was one moment that made a tremendous impact on who I am today.

At the time, I was a marketing planning specialist, which at first was a dream come true. The strategic planning, attention to detail needed, and continuous challenging environment were exciting to me. As part of my self-development, I looked for a mentor within my company, and I was blessed that the vice president of marketing was open to mentoring me. I had been in the role for a couple of years, and at that point, I was doing well. I was even leading the marketing planning for the toughest of the marketing seasons: back-to-school.

During one of our mentoring sessions, as we were discussing what would be my next step, he said, "I think you should explore a role within operations rather than continue in marketing." In that moment, those words hurt. They hurt because what I heard was *I'm not good enough in marketing to continue growing.* And while I let that negativity stick with me for too long, I picked myself back up and kept going.

Well, destiny has a way of showing you the path whether you are looking for it or not. As I was about to start job searching, I was contacted by a past coworker, and a couple of interviews later, I received a job offer in operations as a senior service specialist. The kicker was that this specific role had all the exciting aspects from my past one, plus more operations and new aspects. I was back in heaven! And I also understood what my past VP meant. He wanted to inspire me to open myself up to other business areas that would enhance my strengths. I'm so thankful for his constructive advice because it opened my curiosity to explore new business areas, which led to my professional growth.

4.  Failing is part of growth.

No one likes to fail. In fact, most people live their lives in mortal fear of it. However, failure is a part of life. And, whether we like it or not, with failure comes growth. I experienced failure on a grand scale shortly after I was promoted to the director level. The twist was that I had been promoted to be director of sales, an area in which I was a little inexperienced. Nevertheless, I took it on as a challenge and started doing my best.

After a full year in the role, performance review time came, and I remember it like it was yesterday. I was sitting across from my CEO, and he point-blank asked me, "How did you think you did?" In that horrible moment, I felt a knot in my throat, and I was choking back tears. I felt this way because I knew that I didn't do well. The truth was that I had not reached even half my goal, and as a goal-oriented person, that sole fact physically hurt. Feeling very vulnerable, I told my CEO that I thought I had failed. To my horror, he replied, "I agree with you." And there it was, a knife straight to my heart. I had failed, and it was obvious that I had failed.

As the human I am, I moped around and took the victim mentality for a bit. I could hear myself uttering excuses like, *I received no training, I had no guidance, I had no coaching and was thrown in, really.* I could go on and on making excuses and/or giving myself reasons for why I had arrived at this point. But the fact of the matter is that I was at a crossroads. Clearly, I could not keep going the way I was going; I was not happy, and I was not driving results, which put my job in jeopardy.

Taking ownership of the situation, I sat down and asked myself, "What are my options?" and ended up with two distinct options: I could either go find a new role back in operations/account-management, which to me felt like the easy way out, or I could try to figure out how to succeed in the role. Which then led me to another key question: *Have I done absolutely everything I can to succeed in this role?* If the answer was yes, then by all means, it's time to move on. But if the answer was no, then it meant I had work to do. My answer was no, so I quickly brainstormed things I could do and immediately took action. I found sales-101 courses, certifications, and sales associations. I looked for a sales mentor. I went to the bookstore and got myself a "how to sell" book, and even hired myself a sales confidence coach. I was determined to try every avenue possible to drive sales and meet my goals.

Fast forward a year after that, when it wasn't even the third quarter of our fiscal year. I had already achieved and surpassed my sales target. My efforts had paid off, and boy, did that feel good! Needless to say, when performance review time came, that year's conversation went very differently from the last. The key lesson being that failing is simply part of the journey, and candidly, these so-called failures usually teach far more than the successes. In packaging terms, understand that there will be marketing campaigns that will not yield the results you expected, but that does not mean you stop; it just means you need to fine-tune your strategy and try again.

5.  Make sure you put yourself first.

Presuming you have flown in a commercial airplane at some point in your life, you likely recall the safety briefing the crew members go through as soon as you board the plane. One of the first things they tell you is that during an emergency, oxygen masks will automatically drop down from compartments located above the passenger seats. And at some point, they make the statement, "Make sure you put your own mask on first, then turn to help those around you." One of my mentors/coaches shared this powerful analogy to help guide me toward a balanced life.

The reality is that throughout my career, I have had the tendency to take on too much. I go above and beyond every chance I get, which in turn means that I suffer from being exhausted and feeling overwhelmed as I strive to hit perfection in every area of my life. To break this cycle, I have tried to hold on to these facts:

- It is ok to say no when you are nearing your max capacity.

- People will respect clarity about your limits more than missed deadlines.

- You do not have to be perfect.

If you max out your production capacity and/or you don't package your product (self) strongly, you will end up disappointing yourself and those around you. Make sure you put yourself as a priority every time.

All in all, while you will always be your core product/self, change and growth are simply inevitable. Much like in packaging, you should stay in tune with the market, repackage yourself, and make sure you achieve *your* success goals. You are not a finished good yet!

A native Venezuelan, Jaclyn came to the U.S. on a college scholarship. She lives in Missouri with her Tico husband, Carlos. After graduating from high school from Apamates (Maracaibo), she earned a BS in Business Management Systems from Drury University, an MBA from Webster University, and a leadership certificate from the Hispanic Leadership Institute (Clase VIII!).

Her career has taken her across industries, including food and beverage, financial institutions, manufacturing, and operations. She is currently the director of business development for Packaging Solutions at DHL Supply Chain and sits on the Missouri Venezuelan Association board of directors.

When asked about her major achievements, she proudly shared how, with her husband's help, they purchased a home for her parents and brother who lived in Venezuela. They moved in last year, and the family is back together after being apart for 23 years! The next step is to grow the family.

Please scan the QR code to connect with this author.

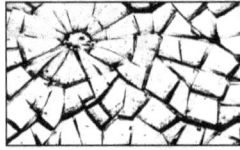

## Saida Cornejo Zuñiga

# My Parents' Daughter, My Family's Builder

There have been many times when people have questioned my experience as a businesswoman. What business knowledge could a 26-year-old Mexican immigrant possibly hold? The reality is that I have developed entrepreneurial assets throughout my experiences as an immigrant. Immigrants intrinsically hold the characteristics necessary to be entrepreneurs. My parents and I migrated to a country we had never been to without speaking the language or knowing how to navigate the systems. It takes bravery and courage to jump into the unknown. I am forever in awe of my mother, who dared to put her life at risk to afford her children a better future. The bravery she holds is unmatched.

We came to this country with the dream of having the opportunity for a better life. We soon discovered that entrepreneurship would be that avenue. Being the oldest child of immigrant parents meant that I would navigate the social systems and new life experiences with my parents, which included inadvertently becoming an entrepreneur. Not intentionally, but by design.

I was the first to learn English. The first to graduate from high school. The first to graduate from an elite institution—UC Berkeley—in all my extended family. And the first to help my family legitimize and administer a business.

By the age of nine, I was translating for my parents in every setting. I was the interpreter when we ordered food at a restaurant, when I accompanied my mom to her doctor's appointments, in parent-teacher conferences, and when my dad needed help communicating at work. For 16 years, my dad worked for a painting company. Apart from it being hard labor, my dad was not earning enough money to sustain his family of six in the San Francisco Bay Area. The exploitation of his labor was front and center. And worst of all, he was treated without dignity and not valued as a human being.

To subsist, my dad would do his painting side jobs after work and on the weekends. He was cultivating a clientele and fostering his business without even realizing it. At the same time, I helped my dad by translating messages and documents to communicate with clients. My father decided it was worth putting in the extra hours for his side business because he was unwilling to endure the exploitation at his job. He was determined to give his family a better life by branching out on his own, even though it was terrifying.

This lasted until 2016, when my dad had the opportunity to apply for a professional license with the California Contractors' State License Board to become a licensed painter. In order to grow, my father had to "legitimize" his business and do everything by the book. To apply, every individual is required to complete a business and trade exam. My father was extremely experienced in his trade and a fast learner when it came to new concepts. The only downside—the exams were in English. This automatically meant that I would be translating for my dad and helping him study for this exam. He signed up for a license course that would help prepare him for the exam, and I accompanied him to all the courses.

I was a junior at the time, and my dad would pick me up after school, buy me a quick sandwich, and we'd make our way to San Francisco to learn about estimating, trade specifications, and more. I was the only 17-year-old girl in a room full of 20 older men in the construction industry. It was most definitely an intimidating situation at times, but my need to support my dad and family was greater than my discomfort.

Eventually, after three tries, my father passed his exam and became a licensed contractor in the state of California—the first in our extended family to do so. However, my responsibility to my family didn't end there. We had passed the first step, but it was now time to learn to administer a business. Now it wasn't just about translating, it was also about learning how to navigate a system—the business world. The same year my father was starting his business, I was moving out to start college. This meant I had to learn how to navigate college as a first-generation student and learn how to administer a business. It was overwhelming to say the least.

But I couldn't not do it. My father trusted me to learn and pass along my knowledge to him. And it wasn't just about helping my dad; it was about helping my whole family subsist. If I didn't do it, who would? These are life challenges that children of immigrants can't just say no to. We are forced to mature faster than our peers because we have to, not because we want to. I didn't understand it at the time, but this experience was cultivating me to be a businesswoman at a young age.

I learned about business entities and the benefits of eventually moving from a sole proprietor to an LLC. I learned about EIN numbers for businesses and establishing one with the IRS. I learned about the insurance necessary for operating a construction business, such as workers' compensation, general liability, and bond insurance. I learned how to onboard employees and how to manage payroll. I learned to draft estimates, contracts, and invoices. I learned how to properly file taxes and the importance of having up-to-date books. As the first, there was no one guiding me or us on what to do. I learned through experience. I learned thanks to my grit and tenacity, and because my circumstances wouldn't let me do otherwise.

I was only a freshman in college. While my peers at the time were worried about their courses and extracurricular activities, I was juggling those things—at one of the country's most challenging schools—*and* worrying about our family business. I was learning valuable skills without even realizing it, not because I wanted to, but because I had to. It's only now that I realize how much of my youth was spent handling responsibilities associated with adulthood.

Because of this sense of responsibility, I had never considered being so far away from home. However, that didn't keep me from pursuing my own career goals. I moved to St. Louis three years ago to participate in the Coro Fellows Program in public affairs. While I wouldn't be as present to support my dad in the business, we would make it work. We regularly jump on calls to chat about bids, scan and send each other documents, and share access to important documents online. We continue to run our business, but now it's not just me helping my dad. We run our business as partners. We are both managing members in the construction company.

Before being an official owner of the business, I never considered myself a businesswoman. I didn't actually own anything. I was just helping my dad run our family business. And yet, I was doing everything a business owner had to do to make sure the company was running. In our Mexican culture, oftentimes the opinions of women are not taken into consideration. We are silenced and relegated to taking care of the home, and that's it. What do we know? We belong in the kitchen, taking care of children. This has been my mother's truth.

While my father was the go-getter, always chasing opportunity, my mother was, and is, the steady heartbeat of our family. She may not have held a formal title or sat at the head of the table during business conversations, but she shaped the very foundation that made all of our achievements possible. My mother is the glue that binds us together. Her attentiveness, patience, and relentless love have nourished us in ways that no degree or business venture ever could. She instilled in us—all of us, including my little brothers—a deep respect for education, hard work, and family. It's because of her sacrifices and the quiet power of her consistency that we have reached elite institutions and high-level goals. She was silenced in many ways—by tradition, by culture, by a world that often overlooks the work of women in the home—but her legacy lives loudly through us.

In a world where daughters are often unheard, I've been fortunate that my father sees value in my voice and strength in my ideas, actively challenging generational norms. He trusts my judgment and my ability to figure things out when I don't know. If my family is unsure of something, Saida is the first person everyone turns to. And while this is a consequence of being the eldest child, the trailblazer, it has exposed me to learning experiences I would not otherwise encounter until late adulthood.

Without realizing it, my father was cultivating the entrepreneurial spirit in me from a young age. Or maybe he did realize this, and that's why he placed so much responsibility on me. In my late teen years, I grew up seeing first-hand the power and agency that entrepreneurship affords immigrant families. My father went from being an exploited worker barely making ends meet to now dictating the value of his work and his time. We were able to buy our first home in the Bay Area during the pandemic, something almost impossible for working-class people in underpaying jobs. But the best gift of all is the spirit of entrepreneurship my father has instilled in all of his children. We are meant to be entrepreneurs, nothing less. My father has shown us what it looks like to be one's own boss, and I expect nothing less of myself. If my dad can do it, why can't I?

As Mexican immigrants, we are socially constructed as workers and never taught to be anything else. It is not the norm for children to grow up wanting to be entrepreneurs. Being a woman adds another layer to that oppression. We are never considered to be our own bosses or to dictate a value on our time and bodies. For many immigrant families, entrepreneurship is the only legal avenue for generating income. That was the case for my family. While it was the only legally viable option to subsist, entrepreneurship was also the only thing that was going to afford my family the opportunity at economic mobility and building generational wealth. My dad rejected the construct that labels us as workers and instilled in my siblings and me the importance of agency. Entrepreneurship has allowed my dad to reclaim his power as a human being. It has allowed me to activate my power as a Brown woman.

To my fellow oldest daughters of immigrant parents—the quiet trailblazers who grew up walking through fires with your families, learning how to navigate new systems without a map, a guide, or sometimes even the language—this is for you. You were expected to grow up fast, to carry responsibilities far beyond your years, and in the process, much of your youth was traded for survival and support. But here's what I want you to know: Every struggle, every sacrifice, every moment you thought no one saw—it all counts. Those lived experiences are a form of expertise. You've learned to lead, to adapt, to protect. That knowledge is real. It's powerful. And it's uniquely yours.

You don't need a title or a corporate ladder to validate what you know. Your life is your resume. So stand in your story. Speak it out loud. Share what you've learned. Because when you do, you give other women—other daughters like us—permission to do the same. You are the expert of your own life. Never let anyone tell you otherwise.

Saida Cornejo Zuñiga was born in Michoacan, Mexico, and raised in the Bay Area, California. She attended the University of California, Berkeley, where she majored in ethnic studies and legal studies, further igniting her passion for immigrant entrepreneurship.

She came to St. Louis as a Coro Fellow in public affairs, a cross-sector civic leadership development program that broadened her understanding of the region. Her growing appreciation for the city led her to join Alderwoman Daniela Velazquez's team as the 6th Ward Legislative Aide for the City of St. Louis, where she spearheaded ward initiatives and conducted policy analysis.

Dedicated to uplifting the Latino community, Saida also joined the board of the Hispanic Leaders Group of Greater St. Louis as the legislative affairs committee chair. Currently, Saida is the recruitment and capital access lead at WEPOWER, where she guides Black and Latinx entrepreneurs through small business accelerators and funding opportunities.

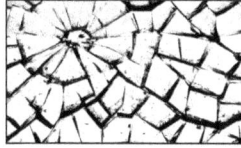

## Cindy Combs

# True Success

I was so excited when I got that call for the interview in Houston. It was for the controller position at an engineering and construction firm. *What a great way to broaden my experience*, I thought excitedly. But I soon learned that working in a male-dominated environment presented its own challenges, especially given that I was a senior female executive in charge. I was an executive in both upper management and at the plant level. As part of my responsibilities, I helped with financial forecasting and analysis. However, during our Thursday morning meetings at the facility, conversations were definitely not always easy, as I was the only woman in the room. While sitting in on those meetings, I was made to feel that I did not belong. There was this lingering sentiment in the room that I would not be back the next week. My colleagues did not welcome my presence nor my input because they saw me, quite simply, as *temporary*.

That was not the only challenge I faced as a woman in this firm. Once, the vice president of operations went a little overboard with his compliments and got too close to me at the copier. I explained to him respectfully that he was a married man and I would not cross those boundaries. Afterwards, I went straight to HR, explaining how uncomfortable this made me feel, and the representative recommended I file a claim. Long story short, he got a few days' suspension. I was not thrilled with this outcome, but I decided to move ahead and put the situation behind me. I remained determined, more than ever, to be successful in this role.

To help build relationships with operations, I started going out to the facility to be present and socialize; while I was out there, it worked. However, one challenge that always arose was communication with the owner, as his communication style was...different. Bridging the gap to understand his needs and communicate with him effectively was a great accomplishment in itself. This man was very quick to rush and make decisions since he worked better in a solo capacity.

During my tenure at this firm, I also implemented a software payroll system that could be used to streamline processes and procedures. At the time, the company had already lost the chief financial officer (CFO), so I was essentially performing both roles. I thought all the extra hours and effort I put in would eventually pay off, as the owner had mentioned he would eventually promote me to CFO.

For the longest time, my goal was to land that CFO role. But that goal took a long time to become a reality. In the meantime, I was actually asked to train a banker they were going to hire for the CFO role. Despite my knowledge, the firm had other plans, and the banker I trained eventually landed my coveted position. My response? I left that company and relocated to West Texas to work for one of the partners in the business.

This situation allowed me to realize that no matter the situation or challenge we face in business, we will always have to lean into our true core values to determine how to best handle the situation. I became aware of the unspoken barriers—subtle assumptions about my abilities, the pressure to prove myself more than my male peers, and the constant balancing act between standing firm and being heard. Yet these very challenges became opportunities for me to build resilience, develop a stronger voice, and carve out space not only for me but also for others who walk after me. I learned a lot about my true strengths as a leader and those areas I needed to work on as I moved forward.

I began putting together ideas of starting my own accounting and bookkeeping business on the side, and helping companies with financials and taxes. I had been doing some side work at Jackson Hewitt and realized the need for an affordable system for people. They deserved to get a return prepared with someone educated in the field rather than just someone who completed a few hours of a tax class. Even though I was also exploring other and more traditional career options, I kept this glimmer of an idea alive in my mind.

Therefore, while working full-time, I began to also work and help clients in the accounting and bookkeeping business. I had no idea what I was doing when I started, but I knew I had a burning desire within me. My dad had run a business on the side while also working full-time, so I knew anything was possible. It required a lot of long hours and dedication to my clients, in addition to creating a business model and structure for my business. I knew I had the knowledge and skillset it took. There was a lot I didn't know, so I realized that it was going to take a lot of hard work, extra hours, and dedication to make sure it was successful.

Despite the challenges in the environment, management, or whatever the situation was, I never allowed it to stop me from pursuing what I wanted the most: to be successful. For me, success wasn't about being at the top but about accomplishing the goals I had set before myself. If it takes a while to accomplish those goals, that is okay! I don't believe people only become successful after they achieve their goals: if you have the courage to persevere and reach for your dreams despite all the obstacles that life throws at you, then you are successful. True success is not giving up even when everything seems impossible. It's the decision you make to keep going and not turn back, even though you see that the path ahead will be long, rocky, and difficult to navigate.

Even today, at fifty years old, I'm still navigating that rocky path. I'm working on getting my certified public accountant (CPA) license while also running my business, doing consulting, and helping other companies. My friends and family continually look at me in amazement and ask me why I continue to pursue something when I really don't need it for my profession. In their eyes, I have achieved enough success. I have a good enough job. I make enough money. They wonder why I keep striving for something that is clearly a strain on my time and resources.

I explain to them it's not about making more money, it's about accomplishing the goals I have wanted all my life. I want my kids and grandchildren to know that no matter what obstacles come their way, continuing to push forward is always the path to take. It is what makes us great. Sometimes we are not meant to get or pass things on the first try. It would probably be boring if we did! I can personally tell you the grit and gains I have made are something that I will cherish. These experiences would not exist had I passed the CPA test on the first go around. The early mornings, the sacrificed lunch breaks, the audio lessons in my car—all of it reflects the grit I've built over decades.

It is okay if it takes you more than one try to achieve your goal. It is okay if the journey is longer than you expected. The real victory isn't in passing easily or quickly; it's in pushing through, refusing to give up, and proving to ourselves that perseverance always pays off.

Cindy is a fractional CFO and entrepreneur with a passion for helping businesses grow, become more profitable, and gain clarity around their finances. She works alongside business owners and leadership teams to provide the expertise of a CFO—without the cost of a full-time executive. In her role as a fractional CFO, she focuses on building financial strategies that support long-term goals, improving cash flow, budgeting, and forecasting.

As an entrepreneur, Cindy understands what it's like to wear multiple hats and make decisions that impact not only your bottom line but also your people and your future. That experience gives her a practical, real-world perspective that she brings into every client relationship.

At the end of the day, Cindy's goal is simple: to give business owners the financial insight and confidence they need to make better decisions, scale sustainably, and achieve the outcomes they've worked so hard for.

Please use the QR code for author contact information.

**Shelly Kretzler-Hoff**

# Rooted in Resilience

Looking back, it hasn't been an easy road. It hasn't been a well-thought-out, perfectly planned, or smoothly paved journey. In fact, it's been anything but that. There have been unexpected detours, bumps, and even complete roadblocks along the way. But as I sit with these reflections, I realize—maybe that's exactly how it was meant to be. A predictable, straight path might have felt safe, but it would have lacked the richness of experience. It would have been, well, boring.

The trials, tribulations, missteps, and even the heartbreaks...they've all shaped me. Every wrong turn and every fall brought me closer to understanding who I am. Each moment, whether painful or empowering, added another layer to my strength, my wisdom, and my resilience. Would I have done some things differently? Absolutely. I think we all would. But would I trade everything I've learned for a smoother ride? Not a chance. I had to make mistakes to learn the lessons that couldn't be taught any other way. I had to endure being misunderstood and mistreated to build the strength I now carry.

But let me be clear, this strength wasn't always there. There were times when I didn't feel capable, qualified, or confident. Times when I doubted every decision I made and questioned whether I belonged in the rooms I had fought to be in. More often than I care to admit, I felt like an imposter in my own career, like I was just waiting for someone to call me out and tell me I wasn't enough. And worst of all, I allowed others to feed that insecurity. I gave their words, their judgments, and their actions too much power.

But here's the truth: I may have once felt inadequate, but I am not inadequate. I may have doubted myself, but I've grown. I've learned. I've built myself back up, piece by piece. Today, I stand stronger—not because I've never been weak, but because I've been there, and I've found my way through it.

Right after high school, I started working in the operating room. I cleaned instruments, scheduled cases, and even scrubbed in on cases. I loved it. I didn't know what I wanted to do yet, but I knew I wanted to stay in that world. I liked the skill and the structure of it all. And I wanted to help people.

As I continued working while pursuing my college degree, I progressed through a series of leadership roles. Each new opportunity revealed a part of myself I hadn't yet discovered—a love for systems, an eye for detail, and a natural inclination toward organization. Over time, I stepped into positions such as business manager, patient care manager, and eventually, manager of nursing operations and finance. Somewhere along the way, I fell in love with numbers, not just for their precision, but for the stories they told.

During this time, I was also raising two beautiful daughters on my own. Later, I remarried and welcomed a son into our family. I wanted my children to understand that while life presents trials and challenges, it also offers deep love and beauty. My goal was to prepare them to face life with grace, resilience, and confidence, and I knew the best way to do that was to lead by example.

I didn't want to just crunch numbers. Rather, I wanted to translate them into strategy, into clarity, into growth. I began to see the incredible power of empowering others by helping them understand the numbers. I wasn't just part of the conversation; I was helping shape it.

And still, something was missing.

Even with the knowledge, experience, and credentials, I often felt like I wasn't enough. Even though at this point I had two master's degrees and years of experience, impostor syndrome crept in. It was persistent. Always in the back of my mind that someone louder, tougher, or more aggressive would always take over and push me aside. My leadership style was rooted in kindness, collaboration, and compassion. But those qualities were sometimes mistaken for weakness or used by others to advance themselves—often at my expense.

The truth is, I had a gift for seeing people clearly. Even when their words didn't match their intent. But it took time for me to trust that gift and even more time to trust myself. I stopped paying attention to those people. I stopped letting their opinions of me matter. I wanted to write my own story.

When I finally realized I did have choices, that I was worth more, everything changed. I realized I was fighting to stay in a world, in a job, I really didn't want to be in.

After more than 30 years with the same employer, I made the leap. I took a role with a start-up healthcare company, working alongside a longtime mentor and friend. For the first time in years, I felt excited. I was the CFO of a mission-driven organization delivering mobile healthcare across the country. The role had meaning, impact, and most of all, purpose.

In 2024, I took on another challenge as director of finance for a local ambulance district. On paper, it made sense. But in practice, it didn't serve me. I felt stifled and silenced. The organization operated within an insular leadership culture, shaped by an informal power structure that prioritized longstanding relationships over merit. It was resistant to change and unreceptive to diverse perspectives. As a result, my decisions were frequently questioned and second-guessed by a predominantly male workforce. Around the same time, I began working as a fractional CFO with Acumaxum, supporting small businesses with financial strategy and growth. That spark returned. I was working with a leader and mentor who valued and empowered women and their role in business. And I was doing work I loved.

And then, in April 2025, in addition to my role at Acumaxum, I joined Planned Parenthood as CFO and vice president of finance, and everything clicked.

Throughout my career, I have served vulnerable populations, witnessed disparities in healthcare, and felt the weight of systems that failed too many. Planned Parenthood's mission aligned with everything I believed: that access to healthcare is a right, not a privilege. That prevention matters. That dignity matters. That people deserve care no matter their income, background, or story.

In this role, I found more than a job. I found purpose, pride, respect, and community. I joined a team that values vulnerability and vision. A team that sees people for who they truly are and allows them to be who they are.

I spent too many years feeling like I didn't have options: as a single mom trying to make it work, as a woman in leadership navigating voices louder than mine, as someone who just needed one person to say: *You're already enough.*

Looking back now, I was enough. I had the education, the experience, the intuition. What I was missing wasn't capability, it was confidence.

So, to the version of me who was just getting started—and to anyone else still figuring it out—here's what I wish you knew:

You don't have to have it all figured out right now. Nobody has it all figured out. Some are just better at pretending. The way people treat you is more about them than it is about you. And if they continue to treat you badly, then let me go. It's okay to outgrow people, places, and even parts of yourself.

You are not too much. You are not too sensitive. You are not too weird. You are exactly the kind of person the world needs. If you make mistakes, that does not indicate you are not smart or capable. Mistakes are part of the process. They don't define you; they shape you. Learn from them.

It's okay if you don't have a clear plan. You don't always need to be absolutely certain; you just need to be brave enough to begin. If you still lack confidence, that's okay. Confidence isn't something you have before you start; it's something you build by starting anyway.

Your path won't look like anyone else's. That's not a mistake. That's what makes it beautiful. Enjoy your own journey and don't compare it to anyone else. Remind yourself that success isn't a straight line. It's a series of choices where you bet on yourself and you keep going. Even when you fail. You learn and you grow from the failures, the same as you do the successes.

Finally, if a job or the people aren't serving you in your professional or personal life, make a change. You are not stuck. You never were. You don't owe them anything. You have choices. And the best part? You're just getting started. One day, you'll be so proud of how far you've come, even if you can't see it yet.

Shelly Kretzler-Hoff is an experienced and resourceful executive with a strong track record of leadership in the hospital and health care industry. Shelly holds both a Master of Health Administration (MHA) and a Master of Business Administration (MBA). With a solid foundation in both finance and operations, she brings a unique blend of financial expertise, operational insight, and strategic vision to every role.

As a results-driven leader, Shelly is recognized for assessing complex operational needs and implementing effective solutions that reduce costs, increase revenue, and enhance satisfaction. She excels in driving organizational performance through strong financial analysis, organizational skills, and clear communication.

Throughout her career, Shelly has demonstrated a commitment to excellence in key areas such as strategy, quality improvement, and team building. Known for building high-performing teams and fostering collaborative environments, she consistently delivers results in fast-paced, mission-driven settings.

Please scan the QR code to connect with this author.

**Cathy Davis**

# Follow Your Bliss

My grandmother Peggy (her nickname for the more formal Margaret) was the second of 13 children. She was born around 1904—there is no official birth certificate—in a three-room wood-framed "house" out in the middle of the Kansas Prairie. It was in an area originally populated by the Cherokee Indians in the mid-19th century during the Trail of Tears. I still have my grandmother's Cherokee Tribal ID card, issued in the mid-1900s. The original structure of Peggy's birth home had dirt floors, no running water, no bathroom, and no kitchen. It had three total rooms: two bedrooms, one for the parents and one for all the kids, and a sitting room where you ate meals and "sat" to rest.

When Peggy was very young, her mother, my great-grandmother Nancy (who was half Cherokee), cooked most of their meals just outside the back door of the tiny house, on a large, flat, wooden "stoop," or porch covered with a roof but no walls. It was called the stoop because the adults had to stoop (bend their heads) down as they stepped up on the porch to avoid hitting their heads on the overhanging roof. Just beyond the stoop, in the backyard, was the outhouse, and just beyond that were a set of train tracks.

The story that has been passed down in our family is that Nancy loved to cook, grow, and can her own crops, take care of her family, and bottle her own plum wine. With 13 kids, I'd be making my own wine too.

Years later, that stoop area of the home was eventually expanded, built into a room with walls and plumbing, and became the eat-in kitchen and bathroom. During the Great Depression, with most of her children having moved out as adults, she became known for leaving bowls of soup on the steps of the "stoop" for the homeless train travelers (also known as hobos). She'd wake up in the morning to empty bowls and, by evening, would refill them and set them back outside. As the hobos would find occasional work, she soon started to find small coins left alongside the empty bowls of soup—their way of paying what they could.

Nancy saved all those coins in a jar. As the economy grew and the depression faded, she turned her love of cooking into a small restaurant in what was then the small, vibrant, and growing mill town of Dexter, Kansas. The small town eventually grew to include a post office, a school, a grocery store, a church (at least two or three), *and* Henry's Candy Store, home of the O'Henry candy bar! That restaurant is now long gone, as is the family home and the candy store. But the memory of my great-grandmother and of the impact she made on so many lives remains.

I come from a long line of women who worked and contributed to the family income or became the *only* family income source due to death or divorce. Each generation had its own set of obstacles to overcome. From the Great Depression to global wars, to the pandemic and personal chaos, the women in my family have always been great role models, whether employed or self-employed, for the next generation. They were known for consistently getting things done. If there was a second common denominator among my many female ancestors, it was a love for books. They were always reading books, discussing books, and sharing books. I remember stacks of books by chairs and on tables. I was always being given books as gifts for my birthdays, holidays, and high school graduation.

After I graduated, I attended Kansas State University, where I pursued a degree in graphic design. My career path after college was not planned. I never started out thinking, "I want to help people publish books." Quite the contrary, I wandered around aimlessly with no clue what I wanted to do with my life. I applied for jobs based on whether they sounded like something I'd enjoy. I was definitely a walking expression of American author Joseph Campbell's "Follow Your Bliss" mentality, popularized during my college years in the 1970s.

As I look back, each job surprisingly led me to where I am now—helping women (and a few men) find their voice, share their wisdom, and publish books.

- My first job after college was at a printing company, which allowed me to learn the process of preparing a book for printing.

- My next job, in retail marketing for a regional high-end bookstore, provided me with experience in the retail side of book selling and in creating effective retail book displays.

- From there, I entered the world of global financial services, where I built and led a creative services department that designed and printed custom presentation books for high-net-worth clients' investments. This experience enabled me to gain a deeper understanding of what is involved in producing a high-quality product for a specific target audience. This is also where I learned to manage a team.

## Moving to a Team of One

"Where were you on Tuesday, September 11, 2001, when the first airplane hit the tower?" For those old enough to remember the 9/11 terrorist attacks on the World Trade Center in New York City (NYC), this question became a frequent conversation starter. I specifically remember driving east on the interstate, into the bright morning sunlight, and listening to the radio as I headed to my office downtown. I worked for a global finance company, managed a team of eighteen communications experts, and traveled a few times a year to our NYC offices. From the outside, I had the "perfect job." From the inside, I was "playing the role" and not all that happy. It was during this time that I also learned a lot about ocular migraines, which began occurring daily at work.

As I stepped off the elevator on our floor, the office was silent. All staff members were gathered in one of several conference rooms, glued to the national news feed, providing the play-by-play of the 9/11 events in real-time. Each of us was affected differently that day, and being in the financial services industry, we all knew someone who either worked in the tower or nearby. For me, it was a wake-up call to stop wasting my time in a job where I was unhappy. I had become a people manager (also known as a babysitter for working adults) and was no longer involved in the creative development.

## Back to My Bliss...Again.

There comes a time when you realize there is more to life than working in a beautiful high-rise tower with a lovely corner office, overlooking daily sunsets. As I walked into my office, I noticed that the artwork on the outside wall next to my door had changed. I had never really paid much attention to the art in the office, as it was always changing and being rearranged. But this one caught my eye. It was a framed "shadow box" of sorts, featuring a highly detailed piece of folded book art. I took a step into my office, and with a two-second pause, I immediately took a back step with the same foot for a better look at the art piece. It spoke to me;

I felt a connection. Now, all I had to do was figure out what it was trying to tell me.

A few months later, I walked into my manager's office and requested a reassignment to a part-time position. When asked what I had planned, I answered, "I'm not sure, but it has something to do with books." I was asked to "hold tight" and wait a few months, as "some things are going to change." I had already experienced numerous mergers, acquisitions, and downsizings over the years, so I knew this was code for post-9/11 corporate restructuring. I figured something was already in the plans. My daily task list grew shorter each day, and I was no longer being invited to meetings. All of these changes are huge signals that your job is being eliminated. Sure enough, within six months, my department was eliminated, and I was given a severance package. I tried not to appear too excited, yet at the same time, I could not pack up my office fast enough.

I officially left the corporate world in December 2003, vowing never to return. It was too structured for my creative nature. It was my time to officially become self-employed.

Working for oneself and following your bliss means choosing work that lights you up from the inside out. It's about having the freedom to shape your days, the flexibility to build a life you love, and the creative space to do work that actually matters to you. It's letting go of corporate politics and endless approval chains, and saying yes to meaningful connections, purpose-driven projects, and the chance to earn on your own terms.

You don't need permission to follow your bliss. You just need the courage to trust your instincts, lean into your gifts, and create a path that feels like home. The irony I have found is that, even in a chaotic economy, working for yourself allows for more control of your own outcome—and income. However, working for yourself is not for the faint of heart, and it demands that you summon that sense of confidence needed to push through a rough day/week. The road might not be easy, but it will absolutely be worth it.

I often reflect on my family's journey from the prairie stoop of my great-grandmother's home to the corner office of corporate America and, ultimately, to the creative freedom of entrepreneurship. I recognize that "following my bliss" wasn't a straight line. It was a series of pivots, lessons, leaps of faith, and a deep listening to the quiet inner voice that said, *There's more for you.* My story, like so many women's stories, is woven with survival, reinvention, and the determination to build something meaningful, often without a roadmap, but always with purpose.

The women before me didn't wait for ideal circumstances; they worked with what they had, gave generously, and found joy in creating something of value. That same spirit lives in me today, as I help others share their wisdom through books. The lesson I've learned and that I hope to pass on is this: Bliss isn't a destination, it's a direction, a feeling, a knowing. And when you trust that inner compass, you'll find yourself exactly where you're meant to be.

Cathy Davis founded Davis Creative, LLC, in January 2004, as a creative branding services agency. In 2008, she expanded her services to include publishing. Today, the Davis Creative Publishing division is a recognized industry leader, having helped over 2,000 authors become published and over 700 authors achieve Amazon Best Seller status, including more than 45 anthologies. Cathy believes it's when we share our wisdom through our stories that we make a difference in the lives of others.

Besides being a businesswoman, Cathy is a Trustee member with Forest Park Forever and volunteers with the National Council of Jewish Women (NCJW). She previously served on the board of the St. Louis chapter of the National Speakers Association (NSA), where she still contributes as an instructor, and is a former Co-Dean of the STL Speaker's Academy. Cathy lives in St. Louis, MO, with her husband, Jack, and their rescue SchnickerDoodle, Chewy (AKA: Chief Barketing Director).

Please scan the QR code to connect with this author.

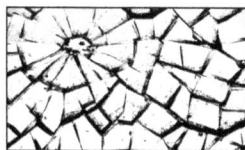

# Epilogue

Epilogues are meant to wrap up stories with lessons learned and end the story in a neat and organized fashion. That is not the purpose of this book. Each woman shared her unique story, each of them as unique as you. Each story showed that there is no one-size-fits-all in life. Each of us is a unicorn, with our own gifts and talents. Each woman in this book is still on her journey of life, learning, leading, and finding her joy every day. They have discovered that no one person can give you joy; joy starts from within you.

Where do you find your joy? What will your journey be? Are you willing to take a chance on that one thing that is burning inside of you? All you have to do is take one tiny step in the direction of your dream. One tiny step at a time will lead you to your goal.

The epilogue is the story of your life that you choose to design. It is never too late to reinvent yourself or restart a stalled journey. We are all here cheering you on with each win and lesson learned. We are excited to see what you, the next inspirational Unsung Heroine, will accomplish. We look forward to the new stories you will share and to celebrating your journey.

Be proud, stand tall, and let your light shine.

—Debi Corrie

CEO and Founder, Acumaxum, LLC

# RESOURCE LISTINGS

## Acumaxum.com

We specialize in helping your privately held company or family-owned business scale through strategically managing cash flow, profitability, and tax strategies.

## Acuma**x**um

**IMPROVE CASH FLOW > INCREASE PROFIT > SCALE YOUR BUSINESS.**

## sprydigital.com

Spry Digital is a majority women-owned, St. Louis–based agency that partners with mission-driven organizations to bring clarity and impact through human-centered digital strategy, design, and technology.

**SPRY DIGITAL**

*Simplify the complex.*

We empower organizations to achieve balanced, sustainable growth through strategic guidance, mindful leadership development, and holistic approaches that drive meaningful change, resilience, and long-term transformation.

**TAI-CHI** CONSULTING

*Human Resource Solutions to Grow Your Business*

# RESOURCE LISTINGS

## exceltoday.biz

Excel Business Concepts champions equity and innovation—amplifying leaders, uniting communities, and shaping transformative legacies through purpose-driven communications that inspire lasting change.

*Transforming Communication into Connection, Leadership, and Meaningful Change*

## krsrealtyllc.com

KRS Realty, LLC is a full service real estate brokerage servicing Metro St. Louis in Illinois. Our goal is to Keep Real estate Simple!

*Keeping Real Estate Simple*

## TDKTech.com

We provide a business-first approach to information technology consulting and custom software development, delivered through capacity teams, individual staff assignments, and deliverable-based work

*IT Experience Delivering Business Results*

# RESOURCE LISTINGS

## menageriecoach.com

We help business leaders get what they want from their business with EOS® Implementation, where leadership teams gain clarity of vision, traction, discipline and accountability, and become healthier, high-functioning organizations.

## menagerie
C O A C H I N G

*Powered by Hindsight 360*